WEBS GAMING SYSTEM

Special thanks go to the playtesters: Camela Brown, Rebecca Jones, Glen Harris, Ron Jones, Mark Ford, Melissa Cutting, Kimberly Foldhazi, Ray Foldhazi, Angie Smith, Jason Klank, and Angela Tammen-Klank.

240 Spicewood Lane
Hendersonville, NC 28739-1343

Copy Editor: Fritzen Ravenswood
Contributing Editor: Gino Dykstra

0001BG

Table of Contents

...welcome to the Web...

INTRODUCTION

Genesis

Webs Gaming System has its origins way back in the distant '70's -- 1975, to be exact -- when an intrepid trio of adventurers found a little white box with the rules for **Dungeons and Dragons** inside. The box was small and contained three brown, covered, staple-bound rule books and a few dice. We were, naturally, instantly hooked.

Soon the intrepid trio had grown to a group of twelve. Still later in 1976 we formed the Role Players of Dickinson Club, eventually thirty-seven members strong. We played every chance we could get! This lasted until about 1978, when the original trio decided that the *new* **Dungeons and Dragons** set in its *new* boxed set hadn't really improved the game much. More alterations were needed.

Only one member of the trio had the time to devote to such a project, squeezing his labors into his busy class schedule. Soon he'd lost track of the other RPD club members, and so by the time he'd created the basic structure for the new game, he had no one left to play with. So he went searching and eventually assembled a truly unique and colorful set of guinea pigs. All had played **D&D** before, and all had gradually lost interest in it. The time was now 1979, and the new world of the *Shamantra* was born, populated with more Character Races than **D&D**, more powerful Characters, and a new magic system.

It was a big success, to say the least. The rules didn't change much (and still haven't) and hopefully never will be obliged to.

In November of 1979 we added an additional power: *Psionics*. It stumbled into shape slowly, taking until February of 1980 to really get the bugs out. This was when the new "finished" game was sent to the copyright office to become "official." In 1982 I graduated from high school and once again had to find new players. These players are listed in the credits because they more than any others really influenced the playing style of the game.

Many people and players have commented that **Webs** allows for more individualization of Characters than do other systems. That was the intent of the skill-based system from the beginning. After all, role playing is always more fun if your Character is unique. If your thief is exactly like Joe Schmoe's thief, where's the excitement? What sets the two of you apart?

In **Webs**, it's a whole new ball game. So . . . welcome to my world, and above all . . . have fun!

Keith Bailey
October 1991

What is Role Playing?

Webs Gaming System is a *Role-Playing Game* (**RPG**) designed with the player in mind. Within the context of the game you have the opportunity to be just about any type of person you'd like to be, exploring strange and fascinating worlds of the imagination. The possibilities are literally limitless. If, for example, you've always fantasized about being an Elvin sorcerer . . . well, within **Webs** you can. So before you begin to develop your Player Character, it might be worthwhile to take a little time and consider just exactly what type of Character you'd most like to be.

What is a Character?

A Character is essentially whoever you'd like to be. There are, however, a number of factors which will affect how your Character finally looks and performs. Among these are (in order of importance):

- **RACE**: The most important element in Character development within the **Webs Gaming System** is probably Race -- the *type* of creature your Character will be -- so it might be useful to take a little time and peruse the various Races listed in the Player's Guide. There are notable advantages and disadvantages to each Race. Also, it might be useful to talk to the *Gamemaster* (**GM**) to discover if there are any Race restrictions in his or her game.
- **PRIME ATTRIBUTES**: These are basic characteristics which make up your Character, such as *Strength, Intelligence, Wisdom,* and so forth. After deciding on Race, you'll need to follow the rules for rolling up your *Prime Attributes* (**PA**'s). These are listed along with the Racial descriptions later in this manual.
- **ARCHETYPE**: Although we've gone to some trouble to eliminate the rather narrow *class* limitations common in other role-playing games, it still is necessary to know something about what your Character prefers to do with his or her life. Therefore we offer the generalized areas of *Archetypes*. An *Archetype* is a basic description of who or what your Character is and enjoys doing, rather than a limited, specific list of skills, For instance, is your Character *primarily* a fighter, a spellweaver, or a computer jock? Answering this question will give you a basic outline to help you choose skills your Character may need. There are several **Webs** game variations, and each has its own *Archetypes*. Your **GM** should provide you with a list of what is available to you.

- **SKILLS**: Skills in **Webs** refers to the specific areas of knowledge your Character possesses. Skills are gathered through life experiences and intensive training. The **Webs Gaming System** provides numerous skills to choose from (more than any other system we know of, in fact). Literally any skill a person might have in real life may be found in or added to **Webs**. Also in **Webs** -- as in life -- you can add new skills to your Character as you play and become better at using your old ones. Skills are the backbone of the **Webs** system and are what make your Character unique and are listed in the **Character Generation** section of this manual.
- **EQUIPMENT**: This is the stuff your Character's going to need to survive the trials and tribulations of adventuring. It can include weapons, spells, clothing, or just about anything else a person in real life would need in order to live. These are listed in the **Equipment** section of this manual.

Each of these Character aspects will be covered in detail in a later section of this manual.

How Do I Play the Game?

Under normal circumstances you play in a scenario developed by a *Gamemaster* or through the use of predeveloped modules. Of course, *you* can be a *Gamemaster* if you so choose -- it's up to you.

The **Webs Gaming System** provides a number of modular scenarios for quick play. **Webs of Wizardry**, for instance, is a Fantasy, Sword & Sorcery game set in an alternative-Medieval setting or whenever the *Gamemaster* prefers. **Webs of Horror** can be set on Earth during just about any time period, but the 1800's through the present are recommended. **Web of Stars** is the science-fiction, space-exploration version, and **Web of Heroes** was created for the comic-book superhero enthusiast. Mixing of the games is encouraged . . . it's more fun. Just about *any* type of game can be run within the **Webs Gaming System**.

A Note on Abbreviations

As you've probably already gathered, there's a whole new vocabulary involved in role-playing games that you'll have to learn. I've tried to simplify this learning process by devoting separate sections in this manual to discussing some of the more important terms such as *Prime Attributes* (**PA**). It take a little time to pick up these terms, so don't expect to get them all in one sitting. I've also tried to assist new players by italicizing the terms when first introduced, following them with their standard abbreviations in boldface. All of the abbreviations will be listed at the end of this section.

Dealing with Dice

Now it's time to discuss an important aspect of role playing that exists in almost every **RPG** system extant: dice. There are numerous sizes, shapes, colors, and types of dice available. In **Webs**, the types most commonly used are the 4-sided (**d4**), 6-sided (**d6**), 8-sided (**d8**), 10-sided (**d10**), 12-sided (**d12**) and 20-sided (**d20**). For almost any randomly determined event or prime attribute, a die roll is needed.

The typical way die rolls are noted in the text tell you what kind and how many dice to roll. The formula is "**#d#**." So if the text says, "Roll 2**d4**," what this translates into is "Roll two 4-sided dice." The first number tells you how *many* dice to roll, and the last number tells you what *kind* of dice to roll. A note here: rolling two 4-sided dice is not equivalent to rolling one 8-sided die. Rolling 2**d4** generates a number range from two to eight, whereas rolling 1**d8** gives you a number range from *one* to eight. In such instances, the game mechanics might not have an option for dealing with a roll of one.

There is a special case used quite frequently in **Webs**. Often you'll be told to "Roll percentiles" or "Roll %." This is done by either rolling one **d10** twice -- the first roll being the tens digit and the second the ones digit, or by rolling two **d10** of different colors, first informing the *Gamemaster* (**GM**) which will represent the tens digit.

Example: a player rolls a ***d10*** *twice. The first roll is a zero, the second roll a nine. This means the player rolled "09," or 9%. If the first roll was a nine and the second roll a zero, the number would have been "90," or 90%. Two zeros rolled always translates to "100," or 100% . . . pretty straightforward once you get used to it.*

Buy Points and Skills

The last two things we should discuss that are vital to the **Webs Gaming System** are *Buy Points* (**BP**) and *Skills*. *Buy Points* are primarily determined by your Character's Race. After that, additional **BP** are gained through playing the game and are awarded to *Player Characters* (**PC**) by their **GM**. **BP** are used to:

- obtain your skills when developing your Character
- increase the percentage chance of using your skills
- increase your *Prime Attributes*
- develop *Non-Player Character* (**NPC**) contacts. *Non-Player Characters* are people or creatures your Character might meet who are not actually played by anyone.

These are usually generated and operated by your **GM**.

Skills come in three types: *Childhood Skills* (**CHS**), *Character Skills*, and *Life Skills*. *Childhood Skills* are given to the player by the **GM** and should be chosen to reflect the *Player Character's* (**PC**) background. *Childhood Skills* are *not* purchased with *Buy Points* and are always considered to be known at 98%. A Character may buy them past the 98 percentile if desired. *No more than six and no less than three Childhood Skills should be given by the* **GM** *to any Character.*

Life Skills are skills purchased by the player with *Buy Points*. These skills have variable starting percentages. How to determine these will be discussed in detail later.

Character Skills are noncombat skills used to flesh out your Character background. There is a list of common *Character Skills* included in this manual. Consult with your **GM** before using others.

If you've never played a role-playing game before and haven't read the "**What is Roleplaying?**" section, please do so now. It will save you considerable time and frustration.

Dictionary of Abbreviations

AG: Agility
AP: Armor Piercing
BP: Buy Point(s)
BR: Bronze Piece (money)
BRM: Beyond Racial Maximum
CBP: Creation Buy Points
CC: Carrying Capacity
CH: Charm
CHS: Childhood Skills
CNC: Concentration
CON: Constitution
CP: Copper Piece (money)
CR: Credits (cr)
DGP: Dwarven Gold Piece (money)
ELP: Electrum Piece (money)
END: Endurance
ER: Elvish Rin (money)
GM: Gamemaster
GP: Gold Piece (money)
INT: Intelligence
L: Large
LP: Lead Piece (money)
MA: Movement Allowance
MB: Megabyte
MP: Mythril Piece (money)
MR:Magic Resistance
N: Normal
NPC: Non Player Character
PA: Primary Attribute(s)
PC: Player Character
PCP: Perception
PP: Platinum Piece (money)
PSP: Psi Power Points
RPG: Role-Playing Game
S: Small
SH: Shell (money)
SP: Silver Piece (money)
STP: Steel Piece (money)
STR: Strength
VC: Voice
VL: Very Large
VS: Very Small
WIS: Wisdom
XL: Extra Large
XS: Extra Small

CHARACTER GENERATION

CREATING CHARACTER ATTRIBUTES

Your Prime Attributes

Your Basic *Prime Attributes* (**PA**) are the physical and mental characteristics of your Character in a numeric form. In the case of a Human Character, for instance, all the basic **PA** are rolled on a **d20**, a roll of 1 being the weakest and 20 being the strongest. So a Character with a 10 *Strength* (**STR**) is stronger than a Character who rolls an 8 *Strength*.

The dice used to roll up these **PA** is determined by your Character Race, so read up on the Races in your particular **Webs** genre before you roll for your Character. Racial maximums are 5 pts. beyond possible rolls for Race. Always be sure to keep a record of the original stats you roll before you buy them up.

PA average for any Race is always listed in the "( )" brackets for that trait. For example, if you read "**STR 1d20** (10)," you would roll a single 20-sided die, ten being the average strength for that Race.

After you roll **PA**, any of them may be increased at the following rates:

- 10**BP** per 1pt.
- 20**BP** per 1pt. **BRM** up to 5pts.
- 40**BP** per 1pt. **BRM** up to 10pts.
- 80**BP** per 1pt. **BRM** up to 15pts.

And so forth. **BRM** stands for *Beyond Racial Maximum*, **BP** standing for *Buy Points*. *Power Points* and *Psionic Power Points* (**PSP**) may not be purchased beyond the Racial maximum. There are, however, skills which allow such boosting.

The Basic Prime Attributes

The Basic **PA** are:

- *Strength* (**STR**). This is a measure of a Character's muscle tone. It's used to determine the weight a Character may carry, how much physical stress or damage the Character can endure, and in some cases, how much damage the Character can inflict. There is a -1 damage penalty for every point of strength a Character is below its Racial average and a +1 for every 5 points above average. The same scale is used for hit point bonuses and penalties.

- *Agility* (**AG**). This is a measure of the speed, coordination, balance and reflexes of the Character.

- *Intelligence* (**INT**). This is a reflection of a Character's ability to learn and memorize information. This is an especially important **PA** for **Spellcasters**.

- *Wisdom* (**WIS**). This is a measure of a Character's common sense and reasoning ability. A Character may have the intelligence to learn how rain is created and be able to list its effects on the environment. However, the Character must have *wisdom* to know when to come in out of it.

- *Charm* (**CH**). Charm is a Character's personal magnetism, presence, or personality. It can be quite important in getting out of certain situations and shouldn't be considered a comparatively frivolous attribute.

- *Constitution* (**CON**). This is a general measure of a Character's health. It also determines how many times a Character may be magically raised from the dead. As with *Strength*, **CON** scores affect a Character's hit points: -1 for each point below the average for the Character's Race; +1 for every five above.

- *Voice* (**VC**). This determines the vocal dexterity and quality of a Character's speech. It is vital to the casting of some spells and to certain skills.

The Secondary Prime Attributes

The Secondary **PA** are calculated from the Basic **PA**. Once your Character is created, your Secondary Characteristics will not be affected by the raising of your Primary Characteristics during play. The Secondary Characteristics are:

- *Perception* (**PCP**). (**INT** + **WIS** + Racial bonus = *Perception*). *Perception* determines how likely a Character is to hear, see, smell, or taste a hidden or peripheral object. There is a +1 pt. per pt. above Racial average bonus and a -1 pt. per point below Racial average penalty to this skill.

- *Endurance* (**END**). (**STR** + **CON** + Skill Bonuses = *Endurance*). This is the physical stamina of a Character. *Endurance* points are lost in combat, traveling, spellcasting, for missed meals or rest periods, from poison or disease. A Character must rest to recover *Endurance* points, and if the Character's *Endurance* points fall to zero, the Character will collapse from fatigue and be unable to defend him/herself. *Endurance* has bonuses and penalties identical to those in *Perception*.

- *Will* (**INT** + **WIS** = *Will*). This is the Character's ability to overcome fear (or other emotions) and focus on his or her goals and actions. It is the force of *Will* that activates the power of magic. The Racial maximum is 100% for all Characters. **PC** get their normal +5% **BRM**. Some skills will add bonuses. Bonuses and penalties are determined as for *Perception*.

- *Luck* (**INT** + **WIS** + **CH** = *Luck*). *Luck* is called upon only in the most dire of circumstances, and this particular **PA** *cannot* be bought. A Character draws on *Luck* to change the outcome of dice rolls.

  Example: Say Ariel has to make a bow shot to kill the wyrm Oborus. She has a 78% chance to use her bow, but she has to hit a very small area on the wyrm's underbelly in order to kill it. So the **GM** *determines that she's at -30%. This means she now has only a 48% chance of a hit. She rolls a 59, a miss. She then calls on Luck to change the roll. She deducts 11 Luck from her total of 31 Luck points for the week, leaving her with 20 points. Since these points only regenerate once a game week, she'd better hope she doesn't have to call on it much more! Still, she does manage to kill the wyrm (poor thing).*

- *Concentration* (**CNC**). (**INT** + **WIS** = *Concentration*). This is the Character's ability to ignore distractions and to control his or her own mind. This is the **PA** that allows **Spellcasters** to focus magical energies to a desired end. It is also the trait used by psionic Characters to focus their skills. **CNC** has Racial maximums, bonuses, and penalties as per *Will*.

- *Power Points (sometimes referred to simply as Power)* (**INT** + **WIS** + **CON** = *Power Points*). This **PA** is determined by Race and is a measure of how much magical energy the physical body can channel without suffering permanent damage. A Character who goes beyond his or her limit risks "Spellburn," which can disintegrate a physical form or cause disfigurement at the very least. Be sure to check your Character's Race for a Racial maximum.

- *Psi Power Points* (**PSP**). (**INT** + **WIS** + **CON** = *Psi Power Points*). This trait is also determined Racially. As with magic use, going beyond a Character's limit may cause spontaneous human combustion, or brain damage might occur if "mindburn" is rolled. *Player Characters* gain extra points to their Racial maximums for high *Wisdom* and *Intelligence* scores.

- *Carrying Capacity* (**CC**). This trait is calculated a bit differently from the others. Add the Character's Racial "free weight" bonus to the Character's *Strength* score multiplied by ten (**STR** x 10 + Free Weight = *Carrying Capacity*). This is simply the amount a Character may carry while traveling. When Characters are carrying half their **CC,** their *Movement Allowances* (**MA**) will be reduced by 1/4, and a -1 **AG** penalty is incurred. For every 25% more units carried, another -1 **AG** penalty and another 1/4 **MA** penalty is given until the Characters can no longer move. Extremely small Characters -- 1 foot tall or less -- have (**STR** x 2 + Free Weight) as their **CC**. Extremely large Characters -- 18 feet tall or more -- have (**STR** x 20 + Free Weight) as their **CC**.

- *Magic Resistance* (**MR**). This attribute is determined by several factors. Race, psions, metal weight carried, etc. **Spellcasters** must overcome this resistance in their victims to successfully complete a spell. **MR** is added to saving rolls. Metal has a resistance of 1 per weight unit. Plastic (being an unnatural substance) has a magical resistance of 3 per weight unit. Other metals and substances will be dealt with within the supplements to which they belong; i.e., Dwarven metal in **Webs of Wizardry**, M'karan crystals in **Web of Stars,** and so forth.

- *Movement Allowance* (**MA**). (Height x **AG** = *Movement Allowance*). *Movement Allowance* is determined by height and *Agility* (some Races have special bonuses and are dealt with separately). Height, rounded up or down, times **AG,** determines how far the Character can normally move in a round. This total doubled equals his or her movement running. Half this total is used for Characters swimming or searching (unless swimming is that Race's primary means of locomotion). Some Races can fly without magical aid, and doubling their running speed allows for this.

  Example: Caith Bellorax is a 6 foot elf, so his **MA** *is 6'/segment (4 Moves). His Agility is 20, so his* **MA** *walking is 120' per round (6 x 20). Running is 240' per round (2 x 120), and his* **MA.** swimming/searching is 60' (120 divided by 2).

Terrain also affects **MA,** as well as *Carrying Capacity* . Distance traveled should be modified by the following factors:

Movement Allowance Modifiers

Desert	**x 1.0**	**Marsh**	**x .25**
Hills	**x 4.0**	**Mountains**	**x .25**
Ice Plains	**x .50**	**Plains**	**x 5.0**
Jungle	**x .25**	**Woodland**	**x 1.0**

CHARACTER RACE

In the **Webs Gaming System**, *Humans* are the only Race used in every game. Humans are also (naturally) the standard by which all other Races are measured. Consequently, this is the only Race we include in this primary game manual. Other Races, of course, are included in the supplemental sets.

Humans have no bonuses, special abilities, or powers granted to them, but they also have no penalties or weaknesses working against them. Humans get 2000**BP** to use for Character creation -- the most given to any Race within the game. As a rule, Humans don't have a long life expectancy: only about 100 years at the most, although drugs, Magic, and replacement parts can prolong life in some cases.

HUMAN

PRIME ATTRIBUTES

* Is a calculated skill. See **PA** description for how to determine this score for your Character.

STR:	**1d20** (10)	**VC:**	**1d20** (10)	***POWER:**	(30)1000 max.
CON:	**1d20** (10)	***PCP:**	+0% (20)	***PSP:**	(30)1000 max.
AG:	**1d20** (10)	***END:**	(20) 100 max.	***CC:**	(120 units)
INT:	**1d20** (10)	***LUCK:**	(30)	**Free Wt.:**	20 units
WIS:	**1d20** (10)	***WILL:**	(20)	**Hit Pts:**	(16) 60 max.
CH:	**1d20** (10)	***CNC:**	(20)	**MR:**	5

ATTACKS:

Hands:	**1d6** (+ **STR** Bonus/Penalty)
Feet:	**1d8** (+ **STR** Bonus/Penalty)
Bite:	**1d4**

Note: The following characteristics are there to help you detail your Character. You may either select your Character's personal characteristics, or you may roll the appropriately-sided die for random effects.

HEIGHT: (1) 5'-5'5" (2) 5'6"-5'8" (3) 5'9"-6' (4) 6'1"-6'4" (5) 6'5"-6'8" (6) 6'9"-7'

WEIGHT: (1) 95-110un (2) 110-130un (3) 130-180un (4) 180-210un (5) 210-230un (6) 230-280un

EYE COLOR: (1) Brown (2) Blue (3) Green (4) Hazel (5) Gray (6) Violet

HAIR COLOR: (1) Red (2) Brown (3) Lt. Blonde (4) Gray (5) White (6) Black (7) Auburn (8) Rd. Blonde (9) Ash (10) Salt/Pepper (11)Lt. brown (12)Dark Brown

SKIN COLOR: (1) Pale (2) Tan (3) Lt. Brown (4) Red brown (5) Yellowed (6) Dark Brown

BLOOD TYPE: (iron based)
(1)A+ (2)A- (3)B+ (4)B- (5)O+ (6)O- (7)AB+ (8)AB-

A Human child Character rolls stats like a normal Character, but these rolls act as the child's *potential* rather than its full-grown status. A child will initially have only *half* of those **PA** scores, and will only have 1000**BP**. An elderly Character gets a -2 to **STR**, **AG**, and **CON**, and a +2 to **INT**, **WIS** and **CH** (see *Age Disadvantages*). Elderly Characters have an extra 500**BP** for skills *only*.

There are other traits which you can give to Characters to make them more unique. Tattoos, hair styles, missing limbs, scars will all help to individualize your player Character. Be sure to write up a Character history, so that you'll know what your Character is like and where he/she fits in. Also, it's wise to get your **GM**'s approval on your Character history, and be sure to provide a copy for the **GM** to keep. This often helps a **GM** come up with interesting story lines which directly relate to your player Character. The more you and your **GM** know about your Character, the better you'll be able to play it.

Character Disadvantages

A Character may wish to take *disadvantages* in order to gain more *Buy Points* for use in the game. These disadvantages often make the Character more interesting and more fun to play. I always encourage players to take a few disadvantages. These can *only* be taken during Character development and cannot be taken later in the game.

AGE: Depending on circumstances, age can be regarded as either an advantage or disadvantage:

Old Age:

- Character is absent minded. +10**BP** per 20% chance Character will forget things.)
- Character has arthritis. Will lose **AG** on cold/wet days. +10**BP** per1pt. **AG** lost
- Character has a reputation as a dotard and is not taken seriously. +5**BP** per 10% chance of bad reaction from others

Youth:

- Character has a reputation as a kid and is not taken seriously. +5**BP** per 10% chance of bad reaction from others
- Character has trouble keeping his/her attention on what is going on. +10**BP** per 20% chance of being distracted in a given situation

BERSERK/RAGE: A Character with this *disadvantage* goes into a killer rage in which he or she is unable to tell friend from foe, automatically attacking whomever is in range until all possible victims are either dead or unconscious. A Character with this disadvantage must specify what triggers the rage.

Injury:

- Character goes berserk whenever injured for 20pt. or more +20**BP**
- Character goes berserk whenever injured for 10pt. or more +30**BP**
- Character goes berserk whenever injured for 5pt. or more +50**BP**
- Character goes berserk whenever injured -- even if it is only for 1pt. of damage +100**BP**

Note: Berserker rage occurs *only* if the Character takes the damage -- not if it is absorbed by armor. Berserker Characters do not make good allies (naturally).

Other: Character is triggered by the death of friends, people screaming, open fires, etc. If the stimulus is:

- Slim +20**BP**
- Rare +30**BP**
- Uncommon +50**BP**
- Common +100**BP**

DEPENDENCE: A Character with this *disadvantage* is dependent upon a substance or an item, and his/her functioning is impaired without it. *Buy Points* will be determined by how severe the Character's reaction is to having to do without it.

Death:

- Character will die within 1 year without substance or item +5**BP**
- Character will die *within 1 month* without substance or item +10**BP**
- Character will die *within 1 week* without substance or item +20**BP**
- Character will die *within 1 day* without substance or item +30**BP**
- Character will die *within 10 hours* without substance or item +50**BP**
- Character will die *within an hour* without substance or item +100**BP**

Impaired: The Character will lose the function of a major **PA** (**STR**, **AG**, **CON**, **INT**, **WIS**, etc.) an organ, or a sense (vision, hearing, etc.) if the substance is not available. If loss is to be permanent, use the time scale and points gained from the list for death. If temporary, only 1/2 the points are gained and it will take 1 day to 1 month per **CON** point to regain the function.

Characters gain extra *Buy Points* if they are dependent upon an *item* that is:

- Common +5**BP**
- Uncommon +10**BP**
- Rare +20**BP**
- One-of-a-kind +50**BP**

Characters gain extra *Buy Points* if they are dependent upon a *substance* that is:

- Common +5**BP**
- Uncommon +20**BP**
- Rare +30**BP**
- Slim +50**BP**

Also, the expense of obtaining the item or substance may give you extra **BP**. Check with the **GM** for details.

Note: It is possible to combine both *Death* and *Impairment disadvantages* to obtain both sets of *Buy Points* for a specific addiction.

DEPENDENT(S): Character has a *Non-Player Character* (**NPC**) who relies on him or her in some fashion. This **NPC** will get into trouble or require the *Player Character* to do things for him or her, and for whatever reasons the *Player Character* is not in a position to refuse.

If the **NPC**'s need of the Character is :

- Slim +10**BP**
- Rare +20**BP**
- Uncommon +30**BP**
- Common +50**BP**
- Constant +100**BP**

Characters may have more than one dependent, which can lead to real headaches for the Character and the party with whom he or she travels with.

DISTINCTIVE FEATURES: These should be determined by the *Player Character*, and it is quite possible to have more than one distinctive feature and get *Buy Points* for each. The features, however, must be unrelated to get *Buy Points* for more than one. Having lots of scars, for instance, will only get you the *scar* feature once.

Concealable: If the *Distinctive Feature is:*

- Easily Concealed +5**BP**
- Concealable with disguise skill or great difficulty +10**BP**
- Not Concealable +20**BP**

Reaction: If this *Distinctive Feature* is noticed and is likely to cause a reaction:

- Causes *poor reaction.* +5**BP** per 10% likelihood of a negative reaction,
- Causes *major reaction* or *prejudice.* +10**BP** per 10% likelihood of a negative reaction,
- Causes *extreme reaction.* +20**BP** per 10% likelihood of a negative reaction.

HUNTED/ENEMY: The *Player Character* is hunted by someone, some group, or some organization. *Buy Points* are determined by how powerful the "hunter" or "hunters" initially are and how often they will likely interfere with the Character.

Power:

- Even: Initially, the hunter or hunters are not much more powerful than the *Player Character*. The hunter has little to no influence on the outside world and normally acts alone +20**BP**
- Powerful: The hunter is more powerful than the Character, has limited influence with outside forces, but rarely acts in concert with others +50**BP**
- More Powerful: The hunter is powerful, has influence with several individuals and small groups. The hunter sometimes acts through underlings +100**BP**
- Very Powerful: The hunter is very powerful and has a lot of influence in the outside world. The hunter almost always acts through underlings +500 - 1000**BP**, depending on just *how* powerful. The **GM** must ultimately make this decision

Interference: How often the hunter is likely to interfere with the *Player Character*:

- Virtually Never +10**BP**
- Rarely +30**BP**
- Infrequently +50**BP**
- Frequently +100**BP**
- Constantly +500**BP**

Note: A *Player Character* can also purchase allies to support him/her in adventures. Depending on how powerful and connected your ally is, you will pay a certain amount of **BP** for his/her assistance. To calculate the cost, check under *Hunted/Enemy* for the **BP** the Character would obtain for a specific power level for an enemy.

*Example: Your Character wants an ally who is Powerful. A Powerful Enemy (one who has limited influence with outside forces, but rarely acts with others) gives the Character a bonus of 50**BP**, so having an ally that is powerful will cost your Character 50**BP**.*

PHYSICAL LIMITATIONS: Some Characters have physical disabilities which interfere with normal functioning. The frequency of the interference and the degree of impairment determine how much the Character receives in *Buy Points*.

Frequency: Limitation occurs:

- Infrequently +10**BP**
- Frequently +20**BP**
- Constantly +30**BP**

Degree of Impairment: Limitation impairs:
- Slightly +5**BP**
- Greatly +20**BP**
- Fully +30**BP**

Other: Limitation is:
- Easily correctable -10**BP**
- Correctable -5**BP**

Note: Correctable means that the limitation can be dealt with without resorting to surgery, magic, cybernetics, or psions.

An example of this is a Nearsighted Character. The attributes of this Physical Disability *are: Constant, Slight, and Easily Correctable. The calculation then is* 30**BP** + 5**BP** - 10**BP** = +25**BP**.

Another example is if the Character is missing one eye. Depth perception would be impaired, with no peripheral vision to one side (Constant, Slight). This would mean 30**BP** + 5**BP** = +35**BP**, *plus an additional bonus for a* Distinctive Feature.

Being completely blind (Constant, Fully) would translate to 30**BP** + 30**BP** = +60**BP**. *In this case there might also be a* Distinctive Feature *bonus, depending on whether the blindness was caused by natural events or accident.*

PSYCHOLOGICAL LIMITATIONS: Character has mental quirks which may impair his ability to function under certain circumstances. The *Buy Points* are determined by type, intensity, and frequency of the limitation.

Type:
- Personality: This Character has unpleasant or annoying habits/traits/compulsions (for example, talks all the time, never takes a bath, smokes, pops his knuckles, etc.). +10**BP**
- Moral/Code: The Character has limiting codes of conduct which he will avoid breaking (i.e., will not kill, will not strike from behind, will not strike or harm children, etc.) +20**BP**
- Fear/Hatred: The Character has an irrational fear or hatred of something (i.e., fear of heights, hatred of trolls, fear of spiders, etc.). +50**BP**

Intensity:
- Modest (the situation is easily controlled or rarely occurs) -10**BP**
- Moderate (the situation takes a **WILL** roll to control) 0**BP** -- unless **WILL** penalties are taken, then a +5**BP** per -10% to **WILL**
- Strong (the Character takes an irrational action in the situation). A **WILL** roll must be made at 1/2 of the normal **WILL** roll. +20**BP**. If penalties to **WILL** are added, +10**BP** per -10% to **WILL**
- Total (the Character *always* becomes irrational and totally useless in such a situation) +50**BP**

Frequency:
- Slim (the situation almost never occurs) -10**BP**
- Rare (the situation occurs once in a while) -5**BP**
- Uncommon (the situation may happen several times in a given month, but not every day) +5**BP**
- Common (the situation pops up almost every day) +10**BP**
- Constant (the situation comes up several times a day every day.) +20**BP**

An example of a Psychological Limitation *would be a person with a case of* Claustrophobia. *If the problem was relatively mild (Fear/Moderate/Uncommon), then the equation might be* 50**BP** + 0**BP** + 5**BP** = +55**BP**.

If the Character's reaction was stronger (Fear/Strong/Uncommon), the equation might be 50**BP** + 20**BP** + 5**BP** = +75**BP**.

If this unfortunate person happened to also live in caves or tunnels (Fear/Strong/ Constant), then the equation might read as 50**BP** + 20**BP** + 20**BP** = +90**BP**.

REPUTATION: Character has a reputation which causes a negative reaction in others. The Character will be known and disliked, feared, shunned, laughed at, etc.

Frequency: Character's likelihood of encountering a negative reaction is:
- Slim -5**BP**
- Rare +5**BP**
- Uncommon +10**BP**
- Common +20**BP**
- Constant +30**BP**

Reaction: Character is:
- Disliked 50% of the time +20**BP**
- Always disliked +50**BP**
- Shunned or ignored 50% of the time +20**BP**
- Shunned or ignored all of the time +50**BP**
- Feared by others 50% of the time +20**BP**
- Feared by others all of the time. +50**BP**
- Laughed at 50% of the time +10**BP**
- Laughed at all of the time. +20**BP**

Area: Area in which a negative reaction to the Character is likely to occur is limited to:
- Roughly 10 square miles -30**BP**
- Roughly 25 square miles -20**BP**
- Roughly 50 square miles -10**BP**
- Roughly100 square miles +10**BP**
- Roughly 500 square miles +30**BP**

- Roughly 1000 square miles, a large island or most towns and cities +50**BP**
- Most towns or cities on a given continent +100**BP**
- All towns or cities on a given continent +200**BP**
- All towns or cities on a given planet +500**BP**

WEAKNESS: Character has a susceptibility or vulnerability to something which other members of his or her Race do not have. The severity of the reaction and the frequency of exposure determine how many *Buy Points* a Character can obtain.

Reaction:
- Mild (Character experiences some discomfort but is not impaired). Examples are a stuffy nose, rash, etc.+5**BP**
- Moderate (Character is impaired in some fashion unless a saving roll is mad.) +10**BP**
- Strong (Character is impaired and must make saving rolls with a penalty) +20**BP**
- Total (Character is impaired with no saving roll) +50**BP**

Impairment:
- Mild (Character is temporarily or partially deprived of one of his senses) +20**BP**
- Strong (Character takes extra damage, or loses one of his senses for a month) +30**BP** + 5**BP** per pt. extra damage
- Total (Character takes double damage, permanently loses one of his senses, has difficulty with healing, or is unable to heal damage) +50**BP**
- Death (Character will die from a reaction to this substance) +100**BP** +5**BP** per 10% penalties to saving rolls

Frequency:
- Slim (substance rarely encountered) 0**BP**
- Rare (substance is not easily encountered or come by) +5**BP**
- Uncommon (substance can sometimes be encountered) +10**BP**
- Common (substance is easily encountered) +30**BP**
- Constant (substance can be encountered virtually anywhere) +50**BP**

Example: Your Character has a weakness to silver which causes pain, blurred vision and +3 damage (Mild/Strong/ Common). Your equation would be 5**BP** + 30**BP** + 30**BP** + 5**BP** extra damage = +70**BP**. *As always, be sure to check with your* **GM** *when setting Character weaknesses.*

THE WEBS SKILL SYSTEM

In **Webs,** your Character skills are purchased with *Buy Points*, which are calculated by your Race and any additions or subtractions determined for your Character by the **GM**. We include two different systems for calculating your skill percentages, each of which has its up sides and down sides. Which system you use will be determined by the **GM.**

We make no recommendations as to which system you should use -- that's strictly up to you. However, we *do* suggest that once you decide on a system of use, you remain consistent.

In either system, whenever a Character attempts to use a *skill* he or she must roll the *Base* % or less on percentage dice. A roll of the skill's Base Percentage or less constitutes a successful use of that skill.

A roll of 99 or 00 (100) means the Character must roll again and add the new percentage to the old for a total percentage roll. This almost always results in failure.

If the Character rolls 99 or 00 *again* it is necessary to roll once more -- adding this score to the percentage roll and so forth. Failure to use certain skills (i.e., *weapon skills*, or *demolition*) can have disastrous or even fatal results.

System 1:
The Easy Way

Most players and **GM**s consider this the easier system to use. As with both systems, you purchase your *skills* with *Buy Points*. However, in this system all *skills* start with a *Base Percentile* of 50%. You then check the required **PA** associated with the skill.

If you're above the Racial average in that **PA,** you then add that number of points to your Base score.

*Example: Channi is a Human Thief. She wants to have the Charm/Con skill. She looks up the skill and finds that it costs 20***BP***. She pays the 20***BP** *and has the skill at 50%. She then checks her* **CH** *Prime Attribute and sees that it's a 15, which is 5 points above the Racial average for Humans of 10. She adds the 5 to her Base Percentile for that skill, giving her a 55%. If, on the other hand, her* **PA** *had been 9, she would have had to subtract a point from her skill, which would then stand at 49%. In either case, she can now buy up this skill's percentile at the normal 3***BP** *per 1pt.*

In order to purchase a skill which has another skill as a prerequisite, you must have the *Primary* skill at 50% or better in order to add on the addendum skill. There is a 10pt.-per-prerequisite cost reduction if you purchase addendum skills.

Example: Lets say Channi decides she wants Acting *as a skill. Acting has* Performance *as a prerequisite, and* Performance *has* Charm/Con *as a prerequisite. So first Channi buys* Charm/Con *for 20**BP**. With her15* **CH** Prime Attribute, *she will have the* Charm/Con *skill at 55%. She then buys* Performance *for 20**BP** rather than its normal 30**BP** cost, and since it is also is a* **CH** Prime Attribute, *its percentile will also stand at 55%. Lastly, she buys* Acting *for 40**BP** rather than the usual 50**BP** and has this skill at 55% as well, since it is also* **CH** *based. Channi now adds this skill to its prerequisites and divides by the number of prerequisites to determine her overall effectiveness (55 + 55 + 55 = 165 divided by 3 = 55%).*

Childhood Skills are not purchased and do not count toward the purchase of *Life Skills*, even if the **CHS** is a prerequisite.

System 2:
The Nitpicker's Way

In this system, the *cost* of a skill helps determine the Base Percentile. Some skills cost more **BP** than others, and that figures into the equation. This cost plus the **PA** (needed to best use the skill in question) equals the Base Percentile. Therefore, the more expensive a skill is to buy, the higher the Base Percentile you're starting off with.

As in the other system, your Base % or less is what you need to roll for success. If you've got the *Buy Points* to spend, you can adjust your skill percentage to give you a better chance of successfully using it.

Example: Your Character wants to have Charm/Con *as a skill. You look this up in the manual and see that* Charm/Con *costs 20**BP** and has a* **CH** Prime Attribute *listing. Your Character uses 20**BP** to buy the skill and adds her* **PA** *(in this case, say 16). So 20 + 16 = 36. Your Character would have a base 36% chance to* Charm *or* Con *someone. You also note that* Charm/Con *has a 1**BP**-per-1 pt. "buy ratio." In other words, you can buy percentage points to add to your skill. By spending another 20**BP**, you can increase your Base Percentile to 56% (36 + 20 = 56).*

In this system, certain skills are also used as prerequisites for *other* skills. However, prerequisites give bonuses to Base Percentiles as well as reducing buying costs for higher-level skills.

Example: Your Character wants to buy Acting *as a skill. You see that* Acting *has* Performance *as a prerequisite, and* Performance *has* Charm/Con *as a prerequisite. So first your Character must buy* Charm/Con *to a minimum of 50% (assuming this is our friend with the 16* **PA** *again). This will cost 20**BP** for the* Charm/Con *skill itself, plus an additional 14**BP** to "boost" it to 50%.* Performance *costs 30**BP** and is also a* **CH** Prime Attribute. *Since you already have* Charm/Con, *you may buy* Performance *for 15**BP** rather than the usual 30**BP** . . . but you must reduce the Base Percentile by 10. So the Character will spend an additional 15**BP** to gain* Performance *at 36% (16* **PA** *score + 30**BP** for skill's original cost -10 for prerequisite buy = 36%).*

Performance *has a 2**BP**-per-1pt. buy ratio, so an additional 28**BP** will be spent to bring it up to 50%. Now the Character can purchase* Acting *for 25**BP** rather than the usual 50**BP**. The Character will have the skill* Acting *at 56% (16 + 50 - 10 = 56).*

There is also a "trickle down" boost which occurs in these situations. Each time you buy a skill with prerequisites, the prerequisites are *also* boosted by 5%. So when your Character purchased *Performance*, the *Charm/Con* skill was increased by 5% to become 55%. When *Acting* was purchased, the *Performance* skill was boosted by 5% *plus* the *Charm/Con* skill was boosted an additional 5%, to a total of 60%. These effects are cumulative, so it's quite possible to have skills well in excess of 100%. This can become useful, since there are certain percentile penalties associated with using certain skills in certain situations.

Another way to purchase skills is through "package deals" which your **GM** might offer. Some such packages are included with each Game Supplement.

As in real life, failure to use a skill will result in loss of proficiency. A Character loses 10% proficiency for each Game year that passes in which the skill is not used, but the skill will never drop below 10% no matter how long the skill remains unused. Physical injuries or age may also impair skills, and the **GM** will have to make determinations in each case.

Childhood Skills are lost more slowly. A Character loses 10% proficiency for every *five* Game years that pass.

TYPES OF SKILLS

Skills are divided into three major types:

- *CHILDHOOD SKILLS:* These are skills your Character would normally pick up during his or her childhood. These skills are mainly determined by the environment your Character grew up in, and what experiences your Character would be likely to have had in that environment.
- *CHARACTER SKILLS*: These are skills your Character might have "picked up" along the way. Although these skills can be useful, they're also there to "add a little color" to your Character.
- *LIFE SKILLS*: These are skills your Character deliberately sought to learn. Your Character might have received some training or schooling for these skills, or worked under a master in order to achieve a certain level of expertise.

Childhood Skills

These skills always are given at a Base 90% +/- Racial maximum **PA** bonuses or penalties. These will vary from Character to Character and must make sense based on the Character's childhood. The **GM** must approve all Character histories and *Childhood Skills*. The different game supplements to **Webs** grant different numbers of *Childhood Skills* based on the campaign setting. Check with these rules and your **GM** before deciding on *Childhood skills*.

Note: Speaking your native tongue is always a *Childhood Skill* and does not count against your total. These skills do not count toward the purchase of *Life Skills* even if a prerequisite.

Character Skills

These skills are used to add flavor to your Character. They only cost 1**BP** to buy at 90% and may be bought up at a 1**BP** per 1pt. buy ratio. These skills include:

Astrology, Basket Weaving, Begging, Bicycle, Bonsai, Card Reading, Calligraphy, Cash Register Operation, Collecting (stamps, coins, toys, etc.), Flower Arranging, Interior Decorating, Macrame, Net Making, Palmistry, Roller Skates/Blades,Skateboard, Stable Hand, Weaving, and Whistling.

Check with your **GM** for any other skills you might like. Some **GM**s will let you buy *Life Skills* as *Character Skills* if they are noncombat skills: for example, **Cooking, Dancing**, and so forth. However, the buy ratios remain the same as if you'd purchased them as *Life Skills*.

Life Skills

These are the skills your Character purchases from the *Skills List* with *Buy Points*. Some skills are not available to your Character depending on game setting, your Character's place of birth, and so forth. Please consult with your **GM** when buying skills.

Example: Astronavigation *is an available skill but would not be appropriate for a Fantasy/Sword & Sorcery campaign. It is, however, quite appropriate for a* ***Web of Stars*** *Character on a pre-tech planet that uses magic. So consultation with your* **GM** *is essential.*

Learning New Skills

INT and **WIS** determine how long it takes for a Character to learn new skills, or even if he or she *can* learn a skill. (**INT** + **WIS** + required **PA** = Base % *capability to learn*). Characters must also either find someone willing to teach the skill, or have the necessary equipment in order to teach themselves.

New skills start at **PA** + 10 % and may be bought up from there. The Character's **INT** + **WIS** divided by 5 is subtracted from 20 to determine the number of days it takes to learn simple skills or skills related to other already possessed skills. Difficult or unrelated skills use **INT** + **WIS** divided by five to equal the weeks necessary to learn the skill. The same formula should be used for development of new technologies, spells, etc. by Characters capable of such invention.

Important Note: The **PA** listed after a skill is always the **PA** the Character has when he/she *originally* buys the skill. You do *not* gain points in a skill when you buy up a **PA** later, so be smart and buy up your **PA** first. Just remember to leave some *Buy Points* for purchasing skills.

Some skills are listed with a "per time taken" notation. This means you are capable of taking this skill more than once. Each time you take this particular skill, you increase your roll chances for success in that skill.

Stacked skills are also skills which may be taken more than once, but they work a bit differently from *"per* time taken" skills. Each time you take one of these skills, you increase your level of expertise, which allows you to perform actions which a person with a lower level in this skill would *not* be able to perform. In order To figure your percentage to use these skills, take your Base % + the % scores of your additional levels and divide by the number of levels.

Example: Say you have Martial Arts *at 128%,* Martial Arts 2 *at 100%, and* Martial Arts 3 *at 80%. You would add 128 + 100 + 80 = 308. Since 308 divided by 3 = 102.66, the Character would have 103% to use all* Martial Arts *Bonuses.*

CHARACTER SKILLS

WEBS SKILLS LIST

For ease of use, the areas in these skill listings in brackets contain the following information in sequence:

1. The cost of the skill in *Buy Points* (**BP**)
2. The Character's *Prime Attribute* (**PA**), if any, the skill is based on
3. The cost for each percentage point increase in skill use (not always permitted)
4. Prerequisite skills, if any, needed before you can buy this skill

ACCOUNTING: (20**BP**, **INT**, 2**BP**/1pt., *Math*) This skill allows a Character to keep accurate records of expenses. It also allows a Character to find and recognize errors in such financial records.

ACROBATICS: (30**BP**, **AG**, 3**BP**/1pt., *Balance*) The ability to make in-air maneuvers, swing from objects, tumble and roll. Also allows a Character to reduce fall damage by 1pt. per 10% to a maximum of 10pts.

ACTING: (50**BP**, **CH**, 3**BP**/1pt., *Charm/Con + Performance*) Is used to impersonate others, devise a new and believable identity, and to convince others of untrue or misleading statements by seeming completely honest and sincere. There are, of course, penalties for trying to impersonate a known figure, or type of Character the player lacks detailed knowledge of.

ADMINISTRATION: (20**BP**, **WIS**, 2**BP**/1pt., No prerequisite) This allows a Character to know the hierarchy in business situations, households, etc. It also gives the Character a good grasp of how to delegate tasks, best use time, and find files or paperwork in a business or large household setting.

AIMING: (10**BP**, **WIS**, 2**BP**/1pt., No prerequisite) Is used to direct a weapon toward a specific target.

AIRCRAFT PILOT: (30**BP**, **WIS**, 5**BP**/1pt., *Math + Astronomy* or *Astrology + Navigation*) The ability to operate atmospheric crafts. Prop engine, helicopter, and jet (need to specify which craft).

ALERTNESS: (20**BP**, **PCP**, 2**BP**/1pt., No prerequisite) The ability to notice and recognize subtle signs of disturbance, unusual events, or patterns in an area. Reduces the chance of surprise attacks.

ANATOMY: (20**BP**, **WIS**, 2**BP**/1pt., No prerequisite) Basic anatomy of the player's own species. A player may take anatomy of other species and simply list it as "General Anatomy". The Character will still need *Anatomy* to become a surgeon.

ANIMAL IDENTIFICATION: (30**BP**, **INT**, 2**BP**/1pt., No prerequisite) Gives the player a basic knowledge of the animals in his/her home area or home world. The Character will have a chance to identify the animal just by seeing it and may know more specific information based on how common the animal is to the area.

ANIMAL LORE: (30**BP**, **PCP**, 2**BP**/1pt., No prerequisite) Allows the Character to interpret the actions of animals, to anticipate some type of threat or danger (i.e., an attack, a storm approaching, predators stalking in the area, earthquakes, forest fires, etc.).

ANIMAL RIDING: (50**BP**, **AG**, 3**BP**/1pt., *Animal Lore*) Gives the Character the skill to ride animals of a given class. CLASSES ARE: **Four-Legged, Winged, Aquatic, Exotic**. This skill can be raised to 98% maximum. Higher skill ratings require a specific animal type (i.e., horse, wolf, eagle, etc.).

ANIMAL TRAINING: (30**BP**, **WIS**, 3**BP**/1pt., *Animal Lore*) Technique must be specified (**Obedience, Hunting, Attack/Warfare, Message Carrier**), then animal type (i.e., **Dogs, Birds, Equines, Water Mammals,** etc.).

ANTHROPOLOGY/SOCIOLOGY: (30**BP**, **INT**, 3**BP**/1pt., No prerequisite) The study of native species, culture, and social interaction. Gives a general idea or prediction about rituals or folk customs a traveler might encounter.

ANTICIPATE BLOW: (30**BP**, *Dodge/Parry*) Allows the Character to anticipate where and when an opponent will attack and gives a +10% per time taken to *Dodge/Parry* maneuvers.

ANTICIPATE DODGE: (30**BP**, **WIS**, 3**BP**/1pt., *Dodge/Parry*) Allows the Character to anticipate where and when a victim will move to avoid an attack and subtracts Character's skill % from victim's dodge/parry rolls. If the roll is made, the victim gets no dodge.

APOTHECARY: (50**BP**, **WIS**, 5**BP**/pt., *Select Fetish)* The ability to identify plant, mineral, and animal elements necessary for spells and potions. An *Apothecary* knows techniques to gather, preserve, price, and sell such items. The *Apothecary* will have some ideas as to how they can be used in spells as well. A **Spellcaster** who wishes to research and develop new spells must have this skill. An *Apothecary* is the only one who can get the most mana potential from organic objects.

APPRAISING: (30**BP**, **WIS**, 3**BP**/pt., No prerequisite) The ability to look at an item and estimate its "for sale" value or authenticity.

ARCHITECT/DRAFTING: (30**BP**, **INT**, 3**BP**/pt., *Drawing/Painting*) The ability to design buildings and structures, estimate their costs, find builders, estimate building time, and locate building materials. Also gives Character their skill -30% to notice structural flaws, abnormalities, hidden traps, doors and passages, in buildings only. Characters with a natural ability to notice such flaws gain the skill - 30% to add to their natural ability. This skill is a must for those who hope to build their own stronghold one day.

ARMORER: (40**BP**, **STR**, 3**BP**/1pt., *Leatherworking + Blacksmithing*) The ability to repair damage to metal armor and weapons when proper tools and supplies are available.

ASTRONOMY: (40**BP**, **INT**, 3**BP**/1pt., *Math*) The ability to identify stars, find directions, determine dates, and locations when stars are visible.

ASTRONAVIGATION: (40**BP**, **WIS**, 5**BP**/1pt., *Math + Astronomy* or *Astrology + Navigation*) The ability to plot the correct path for interstellar travel.

BALANCE: (20**BP**, **AG**, 2**BP**/1pt., No prerequisite) Allows a Character to maintain his/her balance on a moving surface, narrow ledge, rope, pipe, etc. Does not allow other movements to be made.

BARTER/FENCE: (30**BP**, **CH**, 3**BP**/1pt., *Appraising*) Ability to get the best price or trade for goods, stolen or otherwise.

BATTLESUIT OPERATION: (40**BP**, **AG**, 5**BP**/1pt., *Computer Operation*) Allows Character to operate high-tech battle armor.

BATTLESUIT MECHANICS: (30**BP**, **WIS**, 3**BP**/1pt., *Electronic Operations + Electronics + Mechanical Operations + Mechanical Repair*) Allows Character to build or repair battlesuits if parts and tools are available.

BIOFEEDBACK: (30**BP**, **CON**, 3**BP**/1pt., *Meditation*) Allows Character to slow respiration and heartbeat, reduce pain, hold breath longer, restore endurance faster (2 times normal rate).

BIOLOGY: (30**BP**, **INT**, 3**BP**/1pt., *Plant/Animal Lore*) Gives a Character a more in-depth knowledge of how plants and animals relate to each other in the wild. Also gives a Character a wider knowledge of what plants and animals exist on his/her homeworld.

BIOCHEMISTRY: (30**BP**, **INT**, 3**BP**/1pt., *Plant/Animal Lore + Biology + Chemistry*) Gives the Character a basic knowledge of how chemicals interact with organic organisms. Includes knowledge of natural toxins and their effects, information on rates of decomposition, etc.

BLACKSMITHING: (20**BP**, **STR**, 3**BP**/1pt., *Leatherworking*) Allows a Character to repair horse and riding equipment, horse shoes, wagon wheels, damaged tools, etc., with the proper equipment.

BLIND FIGHTING: (40**BP**, **PCP**, 5**BP**/1pt., No prerequisite) A Character with this skill is not given penalties due to an inability to see his/her opponent. Darkness, blindfolds, invisible attackers are useless against the Character because he can use sound, touch and smell to locate his attacker. Characters with superior senses gain +10% per applicable sense.

BLUFF/BRIBE: (20**BP**, **PCP**, 3**BP**/1pt., *Charm/Con*) Allows a Character to figure out which person is easiest to bluff or bribe, and what method has the best chance of success.

BOATING: (20**BP**, **WIS**, 3**BP**/1pt., No prerequisite) The ability to use small watercraft. Does not allow use of large ships or motor boats. Canoes, rafts, paddle boats are all usable.

BODY LANGUAGE INTERP.: (20**BP**, **WIS**, No prerequisite) Gives a Character a 10% per-time -taken boost to use *Bluff/Bribe*, *Charm/Con*, *Psychology*, *Seduction* or other such socially interactive skills. This Character notices subtle changes in the posture of others.

BOWYER/FLETCHER: (20**BP**, **WIS**, 3**BP**/1pt., No prerequisite) The ability to make and repair bows, arrows, and other archery equipment.

BRAILLE: (20**BP**, **PCP**, 3**BP**/1pt., No prerequisite) The ability to write and read a series of embossed dots.

BRAWLING: (20**BP**, **AG**, 2**BP**/1pt., No prerequisite) A natural gift for untrained fighting. Character gains no advantages of a particular fighting style, but can hold his/her own in a hand-to-hand situation.

BREATHE SILENTLY/CONTROL: (30**BP**, **CON**, 3**BP**/1pt., No prerequisite) Allows a character to breath too softly to be detected by others with superior hearing. Also allows projection of voice over greater distances or over loud noises, or holding of breath for longer periods of time.

CARPENTER: (40**BP**, **STR**, 1**BP**/1pt., No prerequisite) The ability to make or repair items crafted in wood (boats, doors, furniture, wagons, etc.).

CAVE DELVING/SPELUNKING: (40**BP**, **WIS**, 5**BP**/1pt., No prerequisite) Gives the Character a knowledge of caves: how they're formed, how to set pitons or other items to navigate them safely, etc.

CAROUSING: (10**BP**, **CH**, 1**BP**/1pt., No prerequisite) A knowledge of how to have fun at the local bar or pub, and how to behave so that others also have fun, plus a general knowledge of what to drink and how to drink it without becoming too intoxicated.

CHARIOTEERING: (20**BP**, **AG**, 3**BP**/1pt., No prerequisite) The ability to drive a chariot.

CHARM/CON: (20**BP**, **CH**, 1**BP**/1pt., No prerequisite) This is the "gift of gab": the ability to spin a fantastic yarn and be believed. This is the knowledge of how to win people with a smile or a laugh. Unfortunately, it will only carry you so far.

CHEMISTRY: (30**BP**, **INT**, 3**BP**/1pt., No prerequisite) Knowledge of matter, natural compounds and how they interact.

CLIMBING: (20**BP**, **AG**, 3**BP**/1pt., No prerequisite) The ability to climb ropes, walls, trees, cliffs, etc., as long as there are toe and finger holds. Does not allow climbing of sheer surfaces.

COMBAT DRIVING: (30**BP**, **AG**, 3**BP**/1pt., *Driving*) Allows a Character to operate a vehicle at high speeds in combat situations. Requires a knowledge of how to operate the craft in question, i.e., automobiles, boats, etc.

COMBAT PILOT: (30**BP**, **AG**, 3**BP**/1pt., *Aircraft Pilot or Starship Pilot*) Allows a Character to operate a craft at high speeds in combat situations. Requires a knowledge of how to operate the craft in question, i.e., aircraft, starship, etc.

COMPUTER HACKING: (50**BP**, **WIS**, 5**BP**/1pt., *Computer Operation + Computer Programming*) The ability to bypass computer security systems to obtain information, delete files, scramble files, etc.

COMPUTER OPERATION: (30**BP**, **WIS**, 2**BP**/1pt., No prerequisite) The ability to operate basic computer systems, enter data, read or store files.

COMPUTER PROGRAMMING: (30**BP**, **INT**, 3**BP**/1pt., *Computer Operation*) The ability to read and write computer programs, find and correct program flaws, and retrieve lost information.

COMPUTER REPAIR: (40**BP**, **INT**, 3**BP**/1pt., *Computer Operation + Electronic Operations + Electronics*) The ability to find and repair damage to computer systems if tools and parts are available.

CONCEAL OBJECT/WEAPON: (40**BP**, **WIS**, 3**BP**/1pt., *Sleight of Hand*) Allows a Character to hide an object or weapon on his/her person or in the immediate environment in such a manner that it will not be easily found. The item must be looked for by someone with the *Search* skill to be found (% of the "Concealer" vs. % of the "Searcher").

Example: Urgo the orc has a Search *skill of 62%, Tika has a* Conceal *skill of 78%, so there is only a 16% chance that Urgo can find an item Tika has successfully concealed. However, if Tika had the 62% to "conceal" and Urgo the 78% to "search," then there is only a 16% chance Tika can successfully hide an object from Urgo.*

CONSUME ALCOHOL: (30**BP**, **CON**, 3**BP**/1pt., No prerequisite) Gives the Character the ability to fight off the effects of drinking. There is a -5% cumulative chance to resist the effects of alcohol for every drink consumed. Characters without this skill get only their **CON** -5% for each successive drink. Some drinks such as fairy wine have a -10% per-drink effect on Characters.

CONSUME POISON: (50**BP**, No prerequisite) Allows a Character to develop an immunity to one specific type of poison (must be listed on Character sheet). This skill may be purchased more than once for different kinds of poisons.

CONTROL SELF: (25**BP**, No prerequisite) Gives a +10% bonus to all concentration rolls or saves per time taken. In combat *Control Self* takes 2 Moves and lasts for one Phase unless a save is failed. If an hour is spent before combat, then the control will last for 5 Phases unless a save is failed.

CONTORTIONIST: (40**BP**, **AG**, 3**BP**/1pt., No prerequisite) Allows the Character to move his or her joints from their sockets to escape bonds or squeeze into narrow openings. Some openings will still be too small for the Character to fit into. This depends on the Character's size and weight.

COOKING: (10**BP**, **WIS**, 2**BP**/1pt., No prerequisite) The ability to turn whatever edible food substance is handy into a halfway decent meal.

CRIMINOLOGY: (30**BP**, **WIS**, 3**BP**/1pt., *Anthropology/Sociology*) Knowledge of crime and the criminal mind. This skill is used to interpret clues, predict likely behavior, and to help solve crimes.

CRYPTOGRAPHY: (20**BP**, **PCP**, 3**BP**/1pt., *Read/Speak + Language Lore*) Knowledge of codes. A cryptographer can decipher messages in code, or those written in other languages, given enough time.

CRYSTALLOGRAPHY: (20**BP**, **INT**, 1**BP**/1pt., *Geology*) The study of crystals and crystalline formations. Also the study of liquid crystals, and crystalline technologies.

CRYSTALMATRIX MECHANICS: (30**BP**, **WIS**, 3**BP**/1pt., *Electronic Operations + Electronics + Geology + Crystallography + Crystaltronics*) The ability to build and repair items which use crystalline circuitry.

CRYSTALMATRIX OPERATIONS: (30**BP**, **WIS**, 3**BP**/1pt., No prerequisite) The ability to use items based on crystalline technologies.

CRYSTALTRONICS: (40**BP**, **INT**, 3**BP**/1pt., *Electronic Operations + Electronics + Geology + Crystallography)* The ability to create crystal circuitry, repair damaged crystal tech. systems, or modify such systems.

CYBERDECK OPERATIONS: (30**BP**, **INT**, 3**BP**/1pt., *Computer Operation*) Allows a Character to enter the data webs and information networks via a portable computer keyboard which has hookups to the Character's brain.

CYBERDECK REPAIR: (30**BP**, **WIS**, 3**BP**/1pt, *Electronic Operations + Electronics + Computer Repair)* Allows a Character to repair damaged cyberdecks if the proper tools and equipment are available.

CYBERNETICS: (50**BP**, **INT**, 5**BP**/1pt., *First Aid + Diagnosis + Plant Lore/Herbalist + Anatomy + Doctor/Physician + Surgery + Electronic Operations + Electronics)* Ability to manufacture and repair artificial limbs, attach them, and train people how to use them.

CYBERNETIC OPERATIONS: (20**BP**, **CON**, 3**BP**/1pt., No prerequisite) The ability to use previously installed artificial limbs.

DANCING: (10**BP**, **AG**, 2**BP**/1pt., *Charm/Con + Performance*) The ability to hold an audience's attention while performing movements in sequence, usually to musical accompaniment.

DAZZLE: (30**BP**, **AG**, 3**BP**/1pt., No prerequisite) Allows a Character to spin, twirl and manipulate a specific weapon in such a way that the victim becomes so engrossed in watching the weapon that he fails to dodge the attack. (Hands are included as weapons.) Only works against 1 Character at a time, and there is the victim's **Will** - your *Dazzle* skill per-game roll difference to save.

DEMOLITION: (30**BP**, **WIS**, 3**BP**/1pt., *Chemistry*) Ability to create and set explosives safely, as well as to disarm explosives. Proper equipment must be available to use this skill.

DETECT LIE: (20**BP**, PCP, 3**BP**/1pt., *Body Language Interp.*) Allows the Character to know when someone is lying, and even if the lie is intentional or not. To a limited degree he can figure out how big a lie he's being told and what part of what he's being told is being lied about.

DIAGNOSIS: (20**BP**, **WIS**, 3**BP**/1pt., *Anatomy*) Allows the Character to figure out what is wrong with another Character; whether or not such a patient has a viral or bacterial infection, poisoning, internal injuries, hereditary illness, or other abnormal medical conditions.

DIPLOMACY: (10**BP**, **CH**, 2**BP**/1pt., *Charm/Con*) The ability to maintain peaceful relations between two or more hostile parties, recognize and manipulate existing political powers and bodies effectively.

DIRECTION SENSE: (40**BP**, **WIS**, 3**BP**/1pt., No prerequisite) The ability to remain oriented to true north whether above or below ground.

DISGUISE: (30**BP**, **WIS**, 3**BP**/1pt., No prerequisite) Allows the Character to use makeup, clothing, and other tools to change his/her appearance or to look like someone else. There are penalties for trying to impersonate someone well-known, etc.

DOCTOR/PHYSICIAN: (50**BP**, **WIS**, 2**BP**/1pt., *Anatomy + First Aid + Diagnose + Plant Lore/ Herbalist*) The ability to treat illnesses, perform minor surgery, make and prescribe simple medicines.

DODGE/PARRY: (60**BP**, **AG**, 5**BP**/1pt., No prerequisite) Allows a Character to instinctively dodge or parry a blow without an additional movement penalty. (Where a weapon skill automatically grants the Character the ability to dodge or parry that weapon, the *Dodge/Parry* skill allows him or her this advantage against all weapons, as well as falling debris.)

DRAWING/PAINTING: (10**BP**, **CH**, 3**BP**/1pt., No prerequisite) Allows the Character to accurately reproduce images seen or imagined on paper or canvas. Allows painting or drawing of accurate, recognizable portraits, symbols, or items.

DRIVING: (30**BP**, **WIS**, 5**BP**/1pt., No prerequisite) Allows Character to operate automobiles under normal conditions. Includes jeeps, trucks, tanks, and forklifts (need to specify which vehicle).

ECONOMICS: (20**BP**, **INT**, 3**BP**/1pt., *Math + Accounting*) Knowledge of money, exchange and banking, investments, monetary policies and their local effects, taxes, etc. This person can figure out the probable effects of new businesses, the loss of a power plant or merchant house, the influence of guilds, etc.

ELECTRONICS: (40**BP**, **WIS**, 5**BP**/1pt., *Electronic Operations*) This Character has the ability to repair damaged electrical devices or modify them, if proper tools and equipment are available. Must specify area of expertise. (See *Electronic Operations* for areas.)

ELECTRONIC OPERATIONS: The price for this skill varies according to area of electronics the Character wishes to pursue.

> **Communications** (30**BP**, **WIS**, 3**BP**/1pt., No prerequisite) This Character can operate long -range radios, FTL radio and satellite receivers, and television transmissions.
>
> **Security** (30**BP**, **WIS**, 3**BP**/1pt., No prerequisite) This Character can operate alarm systems, combat control systems, internal monitor systems, force shields, tractor beams and deflectors.
>
> **Sensors** (30**BP**, **INT**, 3**BP**/1pt., *Math + Physics + Energy Physics*) This Character can operate ships scanners, life support systems, and portable scanners, as well as analyze energy transmissions and sort available data.
>
> **Matter Transmission** (40**BP**, **WIS**, 3**BP**/1pt., *Math + Physics + Energy Physics*) This Character can operate teleporters, transporters, or holographic projectors.
>
> **Medical** (40**BP**, **INT**, 3**BP**/1pt., *Anatomy + First Aid + Diagnosis + Plant Lore/Herbalist + Doctor/Physician*) This Character can operate cloning tanks, life support systems, medical beds or chairs, stasis systems, cryogenic systems, as well as find bionic or cybernetic glitches.

ENERGY PHYSICS: (30**BP**, **INT**, 3**BP**/1pt., *Math + Physics*) Knowledge of energy and how it functions. This Character will be able to figure out energy forms and ways to contain them as well as to figure out ways to utilize such energy.

ENGINEER: (40**BP**, **INT**, 5**BP**/1pt., *Math + Physics + Computer Operation + Electronic Operations + Electronics + Computer Repair + Mechanics*) This Character can do general repairs to damaged engines, computer systems, or power systems. Characters with this skill are not specialists and are not capable of delicate, highly specialized work without additional training.

ESCAPE ARTIST: (40**BP**, **AG**, 3**BP**/1pt., *Open Locks + Contortionist*) The ability to determine how to escape (if possible) from shackles, locked rooms, trunks, etc., from the inside with available tools.

ETIQUETTE: (10**BP**, **WIS**, 2**BP**/1pt., No prerequisite) Allows a Character to figure out by observation what is proper, polite behavior in an area.

FARMING: (10**BP**, **WIS**, 2**BP**/1pt., No prerequisite) The ability to properly select, plant, and harvest crops in an area, or to properly select, raise, and care for livestock.

FAST AIM: (50**BP**, **AG**, 5**BP**/1pt., *Aiming*) Allows a Character to aim with no movement penalty.

FAST DRAW: (50**BP**, **AG**, 5**BP**/1pt.,*Weapon Skill*) Allows the Character to ready his or her weapon with no movement penalty.

FAST LOAD: (50**BP**, **AG**, 5**BP**/1pt., *Weapon Skill*) Allows the Character to load his or her weapon with no movement penalty.

FIND FLAW: (60**BP**, **WIS**, 5**BP**/1pt., *Aiming*) This skill allows the Character to find the weakest spot in an object. Characters can then protect or attack something at its weakest point.

FIRE WALK/COLD WALK: (40**BP**, **CON**, 3**BP**/1pt., *Meditation + Biofeedback*) Allows a Character to walk over hot coals or extremely hot surfaces without taking any damage. Cold walk is the same, only on extremely cold surfaces.

FIREBUILDING: (10**BP**, **WIS**, 2**BP**/1pt., No prerequisite) Allows a Character to start fires even without flint, steel, matches, lighters or a tinder box. The Character can also maintain, contain, and hide the fire.

FIRST AID: (20**BP**, **WIS**, 2**BP**/1pt., *Anatomy*) Allows the Character to provide temporary emergency care for the injured.

FISHING: (10**BP**, **WIS**, 1**BP**/1pt., *Animal Lore*) Allows the Character to catch fish with or without tools. Not only can the Character "tickle fish," but he/she can make simple nets, spears, trout lines, and hooks.

FOLLOWING/SHADOWING: (50**BP**, **PCP**, 5**BP**/1pt., No prerequisite) Allows the Character to stalk humans or humanoids in buildings, towns, villages, or cities (not overland -- see *Hunting/Tracking*) without being noticed. Note, however, that it is *not* possible for Characters to follow humanoids which have superior hearing, smell, or eyesight, unless the Character can *Move Silently*,

Breathe Silently, hide in shadows/rocks/ undergrowth, stay upwind, or otherwise negate those heightened senses.

FORENSICS: (30**BP**, **INT**, 3**BP**/1pt., *Plant/Animal Lore + Biology + Chemistry + Biochemistry + Anatomy*) Knowledge of the dead. This Character can figure out what killed someone, how someone was killed, or in some cases even who did it.

FORAGING: (10**BP**, **WIS**, 2**BP**/1pt., *Plant Lore/Herbalist + Animal Lore*) Allows the Character to find local sources of water, herbs, edible plants and animals, and possible areas of shelter.

FORCE FIELD MECHANICS: (40**BP**, **INT**, 3**BP**/1pt., *Math + Physics + Energy Physics*) The ability to build and repair energy field generators.

FORGERY/COUNTERFEITING: (40**BP**, **AG**, 5**BP**/1pt., No prerequisite) The ability to duplicate the writing style of a known or unknown Character so long as a sample of that writing is available. Also allows for the production of fake documents, fake currency, forged passports, etc. so long as the forger knows how the item should look.

FREE FALL: (20**BP**, **AG**, 3**BP**/1pt., No prerequisite) The ability to maneuver in a zero G environment. A must for almost any spacefaring Character.

GAMBLING: (20**BP**, **CH**, 3**BP**/1pt., No prerequisite) Allows the Character to learn and play games. This skill allows the user to learn game rules quickly and, more importantly, it allows the Character to figure out ways to cheat without being caught.

GENETICS: (30**BP**, **INT**, 5**BP**/1pt., *Plant/Animal Lore + Biology*) Knowledge of DNA, RNA, heredity, crossbreeding, and hybridization.

GENETICIST: (50**BP**, **INT**, 3**BP**/1pt., *Plant/Animal Lore + Biology + Genetics*) The ability to manipulate DNA, RNA, and synthetic genes, using high tech gene splicers and synthesizers.

GEOLOGY: (30**BP**, **INT**, 3**BP**/1pt., No prerequisite) Knowledge of minerals, land masses, and climate. Allows the Character to identify minerals and geologic formations. The Character can estimate how secure an area is and what minerals or formations might be nearby.

GRAPPLE THROWING: (30**BP**, **AG**, 3**BP**/1pt., No prerequisite) Allows the Character to throw and secure grappling hooks.

GAUGING: (20**BP**, **WIS**, 3**BP**/1pt., No prerequisite) The ability to judge distances and sizes accurately without measuring tools.

GUIDE: (30**BP**, **WIS**, No prerequisite) Allows a Character to be so familiar with an area that he cannot become lost while in the region. He will also know where all possible sources of shelter, water, and food can be found, and all common or natural sources of danger (10 square miles per time taken, and the region must be specified).

HAND-TO-HAND: (50**BP**, **AG**, 3**BP**/1pt., *Brawling*) Adds +1 per time taken to all hand attacks (to a maximum of *Hand-to-Hand* 5). There are 8 *Hand-to-Hand* maneuvers: **Punch** (1/2 Move), **Block** (1/2 Move), **Grab/Hold** (1Move), **Throw** (1 Move), **Kick** (1 Move), **Slam** (2 Moves), **Shove** (1 Move), **Escape** (2 Moves).
Hand-to-Hand allows a Character to do subdural rather than killing damage if he or she wishes.

Haymaker: (10**BP**, **STR**, 3**BP**/1pt., 2 Moves) Doubles the normal damage of a Character's hand attack.

Tackle: (10**BP**, **STR**, 2**BP**/1pt., 2 Moves) Does no damage but knocks a Character off his or her feet or mount.

Head Butt: (5**BP**, **STR**, 2**BP**/1pt., 1 Move) Allows Character to use his or her head as a weapon (1**d6** damage + **STR** bonus).

Boxing: (10**BP**, **STR**, 3**BP**/1pt.) Allows for a **Cross** +2, **Hook** +1 (1 Move) or **Jab** (1/2 Move).

Kidney Blow:(5**BP**, **AG**, 3**BP**/1pt.) An aimed blow that does +3 damage if properly done. This can also be used by Brawlers.

Roundhouse:(10**BP**, **STR**, 5**BP**/1pt., 3 Moves) Triples hand-attack damage.

Body Slam: (10**BP**, **STR**, 5**BP**/1pt., 3 Moves) Character bodily lifts and hurls victim to the ground. Victim is unable to move for 1 Phase.

Break Bone: (10**BP**, **STR**, 5**BP**/1pt., 2 Moves) Character locks onto a victim's limb and drives his/her knee into it. This maneuver must follow a successful **Wrist Grab/Lock**.

Martial Arts Damage bonuses may not be added to *Hand-to-Hand* Damage Bonuses when attacking an opponent.

HANG GLIDING: (30**BP**, **AG**, 3**BP**/1pt., No prerequisite) Allows Character to build, repair, and fly hang gliders.

HERALDRY: (10**BP**, **INT**, 2**BP**/1pt., No prerequisite) Allows a Character to know the noble families of an area (specify), their crests, mottoes, and colors. Also allows for detailed knowledge of a particular noble family (specify), its history, family tree, and little-known facts or secrets.

HIDE/BLEND: (50**BP**, **WIS**, 3**BP**/1pt., No prerequisite) Allows the Character to hide in shadows, rocks, undergrowth, or other available cover while moving slowly or standing still. There is a -50% penalty for walking, -80% for running, -60% for swimming, and -95% when flying. (% **PCP** - skill % to detect, plus bonuses for superior sense).

HISTORIAN: (20**BP**, **INT**, 2**BP**/1pt., No prerequisite) Allows a Character to learn detailed information about one specific area, one specific group of people (wild elves, iron mountain dwarves, etc.), or one specific era in time.

HOUSEKEEPING: (10**BP**, **WIS**, 2**BP**/1pt., No prerequisite) Allows a Character to run and operate a large household full of servants. This skill is a must for anyone who plans on running a keep or fortress.

HUNTING/TRACKING: (40**BP**, **WIS**, 5**BP**/1pt., No prerequisite) This skill allows Characters to track animals or humanoids overland to their homes, lairs, watering holes, etc. The hunter can tell how long ago the prey passed by, its numbers, and even have a good idea of their weight.

HYPNOTISM: (20**BP**, **CH**, 3**BP**/1pt., *Charm/Con*) Ability to induce a trancelike state in the victim, permitting the planting of suggestions. It is not possible to force a Character to commit suicide using hypnotism directly, but it *is* possible to suggest that the victim is doing something harmless when in fact he or she is not (i.e., convincing him/her that s/he's drinking wine rather than poison, or that s/he's diving into a pool of cool water -- not a lava pit.)

IMMOVABILITY: (30**BP**, **STR**, 2**BP**/1pt., No prerequisite) Ability to position oneself so as to avoid being knocked off one's feet. Any time this would normally occur, there is a % chance to save against it. This skill can be used with an animal-riding skill to keep a Character from being knocked off a mount.

INSTANT STAND: (30**BP**, **AG**, 3**BP**/1pt., No prerequisite) Allows a Character who is knocked down to get to his feet with no movement penalty.

INTERROGATION: (30**BP**, **PCP**, 5**BP**/1pt., *Charm/Con*) Allows a Character to obtain information from a Character without the use of physical duress. Most of the time the victim is not even aware that he's letting information slip out.

INVENTION: (100**BP**, **PCP**, No prerequisite) More of a gift than a skill, this allows a Character to invent new items, spells, technologies, etc., provided s/he has the other necessary skills. Must be linked to a certain skill (*Weapon Making*, *Spell Craft*, *Electronics*, etc).

JEWELER: (40**BP**, **AG**, 3**BP**/1pt., No prerequisite) Allows a Character to cut and facet raw gemstones, cast silver and other metals, and fashion jewelry for sale, trade, or his or her own amusement.

JUGGLING: (20**BP**, **AG**, 2**BP**/1pt., *Charm/Con + Performance*) Ability to entertain others by keeping three or more objects in motion in the air.

LAW: (30**BP**, **INT**, 3**BP**/1pt., *Charm/Con + Performance*) Allows a Character to understand the moral dictates of a society, find legal loopholes, defend accused Characters, or create binding contracts.

LEADERSHIP/COMMAND/STRATEGIST: (50**BP**, **CH**, 3**BP**/1pt., *Charm/Con + Performance*) Allows a Character to take control of groups of people and get their cooperation. This Character makes decisions, influences people, and thinks logically and rapidly.

LEATHERWORKING: (30**BP**, **AG**, 3**BP**/1pt., No prerequisite) Allows a Character to tan and work with hides. Also allows the construction and repair of leather goods such as armor, saddles, belts, slings, etc.

LIBRARY USE/RESEARCH: (30**BP**, **INT**, 3**BP**/1pt., *Read*) Lets a Character find information in books. Gives the Character an understanding of how to find specific information and reduces the amount of time it takes to obtain such information.

LINGUISTICS/LANGUAGE LORE: (40**BP**, **INT**, *Read + Speak*) Knowledge of languages, their common roots and written forms. Reduces the time and cost required to learn new languages by 1/2.

LIP READING: (30**BP**, **INT**, 3**BP**/1pt., *Speak*) Allows a Character to read lips so long as the language being spoken is a familiar one.

LITERATURE: (30**BP**, **INT**, 3**BP**/1pt., *Read*) Knowledge of books, allowing Character to recall writers, topics and content.

MAKE/USE/DISTILL POISON: (50**BP**, **INT**, 5**BP**/1pt., No prerequisite) This Character has studied poisons and their effects. He or she knows how to find, make, or distill these toxins and how to use them.

MAP MAKING/CARTOGRAPHY: (40**BP**, **WIS**, 3**BP**/1pt., *Drawing*) Lets the Character draw, copy, or read maps of an area. This Character can prepare maps from memory for future use or sale.

MARTIAL ARTS: (50**BP**, **AG**, 5**BP**/1pt., No prerequisite) A specialized form of combat which allows the effective use of hands and feet as weapons. All hand and foot attacks gain +2 per time taken. The basic *Martial Arts* maneuvers are: **Strike** (1/2 Move), **Hold** (1 move), **Block** (1/2 Move), **Throw** (1 Move), **Legsweep** (1 Move), **Disarm** (1 Move), **Escape** (1 Move),**Grab** (1/2 Move), **Shove** (1/2 Move), and **Kick** (1 Move).

Backward Kick: (10**BP**, **AG**, 3**BP**/1pt., 1 Move) Allows a Character to kick opponents which are behind without incurring damage or hit penalties.

Circle Kick: (10**BP**, **AG**, 3**BP**/1pt., 1 1/2 Moves) A dramatic *Martial Arts* kick, where the Character builds up power by spinning in a complete circle. Does double damage if successful. If missed, Character loses 1 Move to recover.

Deflect/Catch Weapon: (30**BP**, **AG**, 5**BP**/1pt., 1/2 Move) Can be used against missile weapons only. Allows the Character to deflect or catch thrown weapons directed at him/her. Can stop bullets, but Character is at a -50%.

Flying Kick: (30**BP**, **AG**, 3**BP**/1pt., 2 Moves) The Character leaps at the victim leading with a powerful kick. The kick will do triple damage if it lands. If it fails, the Character must take 4 Moves to recover.

Iron Claw: (30**BP**, **STR**, 1 Move) Allows the Character to develop immense crushing strength in his or her hands to shatter stone, snap/bend weapons, break bones, etc. Requires a successful **Wrist Grab/Lock**. Causes 1pt. per time taken crushing damage (**STR** bonuses still apply), or the Character can crush 1/2" thickness per time taken of wood or bone, 1/4" thickness per time taken of stone or ice, and 1/8" thickness per time taken of metal.

Iron Strike: (30**BP**, **STR**, 1 Move) Is the same as

Iron Claw, only as a side-of-hand chopping blow or punch rather than a crush. Does not require a **Grab** to use.

Iron Skin: (30**BP**) Allows Character to utilize his or her muscle density to increase resistance to weapon blows. Increases by 1 *Armor Class* (**AC**) per time taken to a maximum of 10.

Nerve Strike/Paralyze: (30**BP**, **INT**, 5**BP**/1pt., 1 Move) Allows a Character to know where to apply pressure to a victim's nerve centers to paralyze him for one phase.

Power Leap: (10**BP**) Allows a Character to make extraordinary leaps. From a standing start, the Character will be able to leap his or her height plus 1' per time taken forward and 1/2 his or her height + 1/2 foot per time taken upward. With a running start the Character can double these distances.

Wrist Grab/Lock: (10**BP**, **AG**, 3**BP**/1pt., 1 Move) Allows the Character to incapacitate a victim by using a painful wrist lock. Unless the victim can ignore pain s/he will be unable to continue the fight so long as the wrist is held.

Choke Hold: (20**BP**, **AG**, 3**BP**/1pt., 3 Moves) This maneuver allows the Character to grab and lock an opponent's throat in a hold until he or she passes out or dies.

Body Throw: (see **Slam** under *Hand to Hand*)

Lightning Strike: (30**BP**, **STR**, 5**BP**/1pt., 1 Move) Doubles damage from hand attacks.

Death Blow: (30**BP**, **STR**, 5**BP**/1pt., 2 Moves) Triples damage from hand attacks.

Hand-to-Hand Damage bonuses cannot be added to *Martial Arts* Damage bonuses when attacking an opponent. Martial artists gain 1Move per Phase for each time taken, to a maximum of *Martial Arts* 6.

MASON/MINING: (20**BP**, **WIS**, 2**BP**/1pt., *Geology*) Allows a Character to shape and fit blocks of stone or brick, estimate the strength of a structure or tunnel, and determine ways to weaken or strengthen it. Also lets Character know where and how to dig for metals or gems.

MATH: (10**BP**, **INT**, 2**BP**/1pt., No prerequisite) Allows Character to add, subtract, multiply, divide, and to solve other mathematical problems.

MECHANICAL OPERATIONS: (10**BP**, **INT**, 2**BP**/1pt., No prerequisite) Allows a Character to use basic forms of machinery: toasters, microwaves, lawn mowers, power tools, and other common items.

MECHANICAL REPAIR: (30**BP**, **WIS**, 5**BP**/1pt., No prerequisite) Lets a Character repair common machinery and small engines.

MEDITATION: (25**BP**, No prerequisite) Gives +10% per time taken to all **WILL** rolls and saving rolls. In combat, *Meditation* requires 2 Moves and lasts for 1 Phase unless a save or roll is failed. If an hour is spent in meditation before combat, then the skill lasts for 5 Phases unless a roll is failed.

MEMORIZE: (20**BP**, **INT**, 3**BP**/1pt., No prerequisite) Allows a Character to quickly memorize information (1 Move per 100 words, or 1 Move per drawing, location, etc.).

METEOROLOGY: (30**BP**, **INT**, 3**BP**/1pt., No prerequisite)Knowledge of weather and planetary atmospheres. This Character can give limited predictions about weather patterns in an area. He or she can also determine if a climate or atmosphere is survivable.

MOTORCYCLE OPERATIONS: (30**BP**, **AG**, 3**BP**/1pt., No prerequisite) The ability to ride a motorcycle even in combat situations. Also confers knowledge of hover bikes, fan bikes, and other related vehicles.

MOTORCYCLE REPAIR: (30**BP**, **WIS**, 3**BP**/1pt., *Mechanical Repair*) Allows a Character to repair motorcycles, mopeds, small engines, hover bikes, fan bikes, and other related vehicles if proper tools and parts are available.

MOUNTAIN CLIMBING: (30**BP**, **END**, 3**BP**/1pt., *Climbing*) The ability to scale mountains safely. This also includes knowledge of how to use mountain-climbing equipment such as rope, harness, pitons, etc.

MOUNTED FIGHTING: (50**BP**, **AG**, 5**BP**/1pt., *Riding*) The ability to ride the Character's chosen mount in combat situations and to continue fighting without penalties to weapon skills.

MOVE SILENTLY: (40**BP**, **AG**, 5**BP**/1pt., *Dancing* or *Acrobatics*) Allows a Character to move quietly even when running. Carrying items which make noise or wearing metal armor add penalties to *Move Silently*.

MOVE SOFTLY: (30**BP**, **AG**, 3**BP**/1pt., *Dancing* or *Acrobatics*) Allows the Character to walk so softly that s/he cannot be detected by creatures or Characters which normally can feel vibrations in the ground.

MUSICIAN: (50**BP**, **CH**, 3**BP**/1pt., No prerequisite) This skill provides other skills by its very nature. *Read and Write Music* are given at base 50% when this skill is taken for no additional **BP**. The Character must specify the musical instrument of choice. New instrument skills may be purchased for 10**BP** each and start at a base of 40%, which may be bought up at a 3**BP**/1pt. ratio.

NAVIGATION: (30**BP**, **WIS**, 5**BP**/1pt., *Math + Astronomy* or *Astrology*) This skill allows a Character to plot a course by the stars. It is an important skill for Characters who travel by sea or by land and also for those who pilot starships.

NUCLEAR PHYSICS: (20**BP**, **INT**,, 2**BP**/1pt., *Physics*) Knowledge of molecular fusion and fission. This Character will be familiar with the uses of nuclear power as well as its hazards.

OCCULT STUDIES/THEOLOGY: (10**BP**, **INT**, 2**BP**/1pt., *Read*) Knowledge of a single religion (specify), Characters will be familiar with the religious practices, rituals, beliefs, supernatural tales and taboos of the specified religion.

OPEN LOCKS: (50**BP**, **AG**, 5**BP**/1pt., No prerequisite) Allows Character to pick locks with whatever tools are available.

PACKING: (20**BP**, **WIS**, 2**BP**/1pt., No prerequisite) Allows a Character to pack objects in such a way that the maximum number of objects can be fitted into a space, while also being evenly balanced and securely placed. Reduces encumbrance penalties by 1/2 of the Character's *Packing* skill, up to a maximum of 80%.

PARACHUTING/SKY DIVING: (20**BP**, **AG**, 3**BP**/1pt., No prerequisite) The ability to pack and use parachutes.

PERFORMANCE: (10**BP**, **WILL**, 2**BP**/1pt., *Charm/Con*) The ability to take some form of action in front of groups of people with confidence.

PHOTOGRAPHY: (20**BP**, **CH**, 2**BP**/1pt., *Mechanical Operations*) The ability to use photographic equipment, develop film and pull prints.

PHYSICS: (30**BP**, **INT**, 3**BP**/1pt., *Math*) Knowledge of natural law and energy. Gravity, inertia, light, etc., are all studied within this science.

PICK POCKET: (50**BP**, **AG**, 5**BP**/1pt., No prerequisite) The ability to take objects from people's pockets, pouches, packs, or purses without being caught. This roll must be made twice -- once to reach into the pouch, pocket, purse, etc., and then again to get the hand out without detection. (A Character can also cut pouch strings or purse handles. In these circumstances, only one roll need be made.)

PLANT LORE/HERBALIST: (20**BP**, **WIS**, 3**BP**/1pt., No prerequisite) Allows the Character to identify and locate local plant life. Also lets the Character make simple herbal potions and teas.

POLE VAULTING: (20**BP**, **AG**, 3**BP**/1pt., No prerequisite) Lets the Character use poles to climb or jump over objects.

POTTER/SCULPTOR: (20**BP**, **AG**, 3**BP**/1pt., No prerequisite) Allows a Character to make items out of clay or stone. The Character will know how to fire and glaze pieces as well.

POWERBOAT: (20**BP**, **AG**, 3**BP**/1pt., *Boating*) This Character will be able to operate motor boats and racing boats.

PRONE FIGHTING: (30**BP**, **AG**, 3**BP**/1pt., No prerequisite) Allows the Character to fight from a

prone position without penalty.
PROSTITUTION/SEDUCTION: (10**BP**, **CH**, 3**BP**/1pt., *Charm/Con*) Allows a Character to use physical charms to get what he/she wants.

PSIOMECHANICS: (30**BP**, **WIS**, 3**BP**/1pt., *Mechanics*) This Character can build or repair machinery which operates on psionic energies.

PSIOTRONICS: (30**BP**, **INT**, 3**BP**/1pt., *Electronic Operations + Electronics*) This Character can repair psiotech computers and psiotech systems as well as program in the virtual-reality net.

PSIOTECH OPERATIONS: (30**BP**, **CNC**, 5**BP**/1pt., No prerequisite) Allows a Character to recognize and operate psiotech machines, systems, and weapons.

PSYCHOLOGY: (30**BP**, **INT**, 3**BP**/1pt., *Charm/Con*) Knowledge of the human or sentient mind. This Character can recognize and treat mental illness.

QUANTUM PHYSICS: (30**BP**, **INT**, 3**BP**/1pt., *Math + Physics*) Knowledge of quantum particles and how they react in the universe. *Quantum Physics* is the science which allows for folded-space jumps and time travel.

QUANTUM MECHANICS: (50**BP**, **INT**, 10**BP**/1pt., *Math + Physics + Quantum Physics*) Allows a Character to repair and operate Quantum Drive systems.

READ/WRITE: (40**BP**, **INT**, 5**BP**/1pt., No prerequisite) This skill permits the Character to learn to read and write in a new language (specify). This skill may be purchased repeatedly with no restrictions on what skill level the Character might have with another language.

RESPIRATOR OPERATION: (10**BP**, **WIS**, 3**BP**/1pt., No prerequisite) Lets the Character operate artificial respirators, air purifiers, and oxygen tanks.

RITUAL DESIGN: (30**BP**, **INT**, 5**BP**/1pt., *Occult Studies*) Allows the Character to invent new rituals for magic.

ROPE MASTERY: (30**BP**, **AG**, 3**BP**/1pt., No prerequisite) Allows Characters to use ropes to walk upon, swing on/from, and climb. They can also make other maneuvers while doing so.

ROPE WORKING: (30**BP**, **WIS**, 3**BP**/1pt., No prerequisite) Allows a Character to knot, tie, splice, throw, or otherwise manipulate ropes.

RUNNING DISTANCE: (30**BP**, **END**, 3**BP**/1pt., No prerequisite) Allows a Character to run for long periods of time and lose only 1/2 the normal endurance points (1pt. per Phase).
RUNNING SPRINT: (30**BP**, **END**, 3**BP**/1pt., No prerequisite) Doubles the Character's running speed for 1 Combat Round. Character will lose an extra 2 **END** points per Phase for sprinting.

SAGE KNOWLEDGE: (10**BP**, **INT**, 3**BP**/1pt., No prerequisite) Gives a Character detailed knowledge of one (specify) particular topic-- for example, the Mage Mestromu, Wyrm Maribar, Captain Largo, the crew of the starship Bountiful, flora of Vallen Wood valley, etc.

SAILING: (30**BP**, **WIS**, 5**BP**/1pt., *Boating*) Gives the Character a knowledge of sailing maneuvers and how to execute them. Character will know of several safe ports and have limited knowledge of where reefs, bays, cliffs, sand bars, etc., are located.

SCUBA DIVING: (30**BP**, **INT**, 3**BP**/1pt., *Respirator Operation*) Allows Character to use scuba gear safely. The Character can maneuver under water with no penalties (unless situation is unusual.)

SCROUNGING: (20**BP**, **WIS**, 3**BP**/1pt., No prerequisite) The ability to find useful objects or food in village, town, city, space port, etc. This Character knows where all the best junk can be found.

SEARCH: (50**BP**, **PCP**, 5**BP**/1pt., No prerequisite) Gives the Character the ability to find things deliberately hidden or concealed (i.e., secret passages, traps, hiding Characters, weapons, etc).

SIGN LANGUAGE: (30**BP**, **INT**, 3**BP**/1pt., No prerequisite) Allows the Character to understand and perform a language of hand gestures.

SELECT FETISH: (20**BP**, **WIS**, 5**BP**/1pt., No prerequisite) Allows the Character to sort through organic materials to find those which contain the most mana for use in spell casting. The Character will know how much mana is in the object and what sort of spells it is best suited for.

SHIP BUILDING: (30**BP**, **WIS**, 3**BP**/1pt., *Carpenter*) Gives the Character the knowledge of how to construct watergoing vessels.

SINGING: (10**BP**, **VC**, 3**BP**/1pt., *Charm/Con + Performance*) The Character can entertain with the use of his or her voice. The Character will be able to stay in key and keep proper time with accompaniment.

SLEIGHT OF HAND: (30**BP**, **AG**, 3**BP**/1pt., No prerequisite) Allows a Character to manipulate objects in his/her hands to distract or hide items.

SNOW CRAFT: (30**BP**, **AG**, 3**BP**/1pt., No prerequisite) Gives the Character the ability to ski, walk on snowshoes, and ice skate.

SONG WRITING: (20**BP**, **CH**, 3**BP**/1pt., *Musician*) This Character can create new songs or ballads.

SOUND IMITATION/MIMICRY: (30**BP**, **VC**., 5**BP**/1pt., No prerequisite) This skill allows a Character to imitate any sound or voice previously heard.

SPEAK: (40**BP**, **INT**, 3**BP**/1pt., No prerequisite) Allows the Character to learn a new language (specify).

SPEED READING: (20**BP**, **INT**, 3**BP**/1pt., *Read*) Lets a Character read quickly, shortening the time it takes to research or find vital information.

SPIRIT LORE: (30**BP**, **WIS**, 3**BP**/1pt., *Occult Studies*) Knowledge of spirits, their habits and abilities. This Character will know about ghosts, ban shide, specters, poltergeists, and other such ethereal creatures.

STARSHIP PILOT: (30**BP**, **WIS**, 3**BP**/1pt., *Math + Astronomy* or *Astrology + Navigation + Astronavigation*) Allows Character to operate a starship.

STORY TELLING: (20**BP**, **CH**, 3**BP**/1pt., *Charm/Con + Performance*) Lets the Character hold an audience's attention with the telling of fictional encounters or historical events.

SURGERY: (30**BP**, **WIS**, 5**BP**/1pt., *Plant/Animal Lore + First Aid + Anatomy + Diagnosis + Doctor/Physician*) Allows the Character to perform major surgical operations on other Characters.

SURVIVALIST: (10**BP**, **WIS**, 2**BP**/1pt., *Plant/Animal Lore + Foraging*) Gives Character a knowledge of how to survive in various climates. This Character will know what is needed to survive in various emergency situations.

SWIMMING: (20**BP**, **AG**, 3**BP**/1pt., No prerequisite) Allows the Character to swim.

TAILOR: (30**BP**, **WIS**, 3**BP**/1pt., No prerequisite) The ability to make patterns, cut cloth, and create clothing which fits.

TAUNT: (10**BP**, **CH**, 3**BP**/1pt., No prerequisite) Allows a Character to so enrage a victim that he/she becomes incapable of thinking clearly. This gives the victim a 10% penalty per time for all actions.

TELEGRAPHY: (10**BP**, **WIS**, 3**BP**/1pt., *Mechanical Operations*) The ability to send and receive simple codes (i.e., Morse code), using simple telegraphic devices, light flashes, tapping on pipes, etc.

THROWING: (30**BP**, **AG**, 3**BP**/1pt., No prerequisite) The ability to hit a specified target with an object thrown by the Character.

TORTURE: (30**BP**, **WIS**, 3**BP**/1pt., *Anatomy + Detect Lie*) The use of physical discomfort to extract information (good Characters do not use this skill).

TRANSPORTAL PHYSICS: (30**BP**, **INT**, 3**BP**/1pt., *Math + Physics + Energy Physics*) The study of matter transmission. This is the physics necessary for transporters and teleporters, and it is also necessary for food and item replicators.

TRAP SETTING/MAKING/DISARMING: (50**BP**, **WIS**, 5**BP**/1pt., No prerequisite) This is the understanding of traps: how they are set, how they operate, and how to get around them.

TRICK RIDING: (30**BP**, **AG**, 3**BP**/1pt., *Riding*) Allows a Character to do circus-type riding tricks (stand, leap from an animal's back, ride backwards, do handstands, etc.).

TUNESMITHING: (20**BP**, **INT**, 3**BP**/1pt., *Carpenter*) The ability to make or repair musical instruments.

TWO-HANDED FIGHTING: (50**BP**, **AG**, 5**BP**/1pt., No prerequisite) Allows Character to use weapons or make attacks with both hands without penalty. Attacks still take 1 Move, but can be made simultaneously. A Character may also attack with one weapon and parry with the other.

UNDERWATER DEMOLITIONS: (20**BP**, **WIS**, 3**BP**/1pt., *Chemistry + Demolitions*) The ability to set and disarm explosives for underwater use.

VAC SUIT MECHANICS: (20**BP**, **WIS**, 3**BP**/1pt., *Respirator Operation*) The ability to make and repair vacuum suits if proper tools are available.

VAC SUIT OPERATIONS: (20**BP**, **WIS**, 3**BP**/1pt., *Free Fall*) The ability to use vacuum suits.

VETERINARY: (30**BP**, **WIS**, 3**BP**/1pt., *General Anatomy*) The ability to diagnose, medicate, and otherwise treat animals.

VIRTUAL MANEUVERING/COMBAT: (30**BP**, **WIS**, 3**BP**/1pt., *Computer Operation + Cyberdeck Operations*) Allows the Character to move in the data webs and information networks. He can locate data, erase or copy files, or fight enemy programs.

WAGONEERING: (30**BP**, **AG**, 3**BP**/1pt., No prerequisite) The ability to drive wagons and carts pulled by animals.

WATER LORE: (30**BP**, **INT**, 3**BP**/1pt., No prerequisite) Knowledge of water, its dangers, and how it flows. This Character can find hidden water, predict dangers (unseen reefs, sandbars, rocks, whitewater areas, etc.) and will have a general knowledge of where major rivers, seas, and oceans are on his/her home world (specify: other worlds can be studied) and what life forms are commonly found in those bodies of water.

WEAPONSMITHING: (30**BP**, **INT**, 3**BP**/1pt., *Leatherworking + Blacksmithing + Armorer*) This is the ability to build or repair weapons. There are three types of weaponsmiths, and each type must be purchased separately:

Primitive: This Character can repair simple nonmechanical weapons such as swords, knives, maces, and even bows.

Projectile: This Character can fashion or repair weapons such as crossbows, guns, cannons and other projectile weapons.

Energy: This Character can build and repair laser guns, plasma weapons, power swords, photon pistols, and other energy-generating weaponry.

WEAPON SKILL: (special) Every weapon has a cost to buy and fit into a weapon class. You must first buy the class; then you can buy weapon skills from within that class. The Classes are: **Clubs, Axes and Maces**; **Blades**; **Chain and Rope**; **Pole Arms**; **Fist loads**; **Bows**; **Guns**; and **Specialty**. Each class costs 30**BP** and gives the Character a Base 50% chance +/-**PA** per weapon bonus or penalty to use weapons in that class (the exception is the **Specialty** weapons class in which the Character has a Base 50% with 3 weapons and a Base 20% with the others). A Character cannot buy above a *Weapon Skill* 3 with any weapon unless he or she becomes a ***Weaponmaster***.

WIRETAPPING/SURVEILLANCE: (30**BP**, **INT**, 3**BP**/1pt., *Mechanical Operations*) The ability to plant recording devices, video cameras, and other related equipment so that they will not be noticed without an active search, and to monitor the equipment once it is set.

WRESTLING: (50**BP**, **AG**, 3**BP**/1pt., *Brawling*) A fighting skill useful in subduing rather than harming opponents.

Tackle: (10**BP**, **STR**, 2**BP**/1pt., 2 Moves) Does no damage but knocks a Character off his or her feet or mount.

Head Butt: (5**BP**, **STR**, 2**BP**/1pt., 1 Move) Allows Character to use his or her head as a weapon (1**d6** damage + **STR** bonus).

Body Slam: (10**BP**, **STR**, 5**BP**/1pt., 3 Moves) Character bodily lifts and hurls the victim to the ground. Victim is unable to move for 1 Phase.

Wrist Grab/Lock: (10**BP**, **AG**, 3**BP**/1pt., 1 Move) Allows the Character to incapacitate another by locking a wrist in a painful hold. Unless the victim can ignore pain, he or she will not be able to continue the fight so long as the wrist is held.

Choke Hold: (20**BP**, **AG**, 3**BP**/1pt., 3 Moves) This maneuver allows the Character to grab and lock an opponent's throat in a hold until he or she passes out or dies.

WRITING: (20**BP**, **CH**, 2**BP**/1pt., *Read/Write*) This Character can write stories which are entertaining to others.

XENO "SCIENCES": (30**BP,** No prerequisite) This is the knowledge of a particular science concerning aliens. Requires a specific science to be added to the base skill (i.e.; *Xenobiology* requires *Biology* and is bought up in the same way, *Xenoanatomy*, *Xenoarchaeology*, *Xenopsychology* are also possible). Check with your **GM** about what xeno "sciences" he or she allows.

PSIONICS

Psions are not always available to Characters in all of the **Webs Gaming Systems**, so check with the **GM** and the **Basic Set** rules to determine what psions are available to your Character. Psions are broken down into *Circles* and *Fields*, and each must be purchased separately. Characters gain +5 **PSP** per 100pt. in a Field. A Psionic Character is not able to use *Essence/Spirit* magic, since his/her body and mind will be attuned to a different form of energy.

PSIONIC: (50**BP**) This skill allows a Character to be psionic and to purchase psionic abilities. The Character gains +10 **PSP** and +20% to **CNC**.

CIRCLE OF ALTERATIONS:

(50**BP**) Allows the Character to buy psions in the Fields of **ALTERATIONS ENERGY, ALTERATIONS MATTER,** or **ALTERATIONS PHYSICAL**. Character gains 10 **PSP** and 5% to **CNC**.

Field of ALTERATIONS ENERGY: (50**BP**, 3**BP**/1pt.) Allows a Character to buy psions from the Field of *Alterations Energy*. Also allows the Character to sense such Alterations in use (-10% **CNC**). -1pt. per 10' radius, -1 **END** per 10' radius, 1 Move per 10' radius.

BIOELECTRICITY: (30**BP**, 3**BP**/1pt.) Allows the Character to direct a bioelectric blast at a target (-20% **CNC**). -1pt. per pt. of blast, - 1 **END** per 2pt., 1 Move.

CRYOKINETICS: (30**BP**, 3**BP**/1pt.) Allows a Character to lower the temperature of an object (-20% **CNC**, -40%**CNC** in combat/rushed). -1pt. per degree lowered, -1 **END** per Move maintained, 1 Move.

ENERGY BARRIER: (50**BP**, 5**BP**/1pt.) Allows a Character to deflect energy attacks, laser blasts, radiation, and even magic (-20% **CNC**, -40% combat/rushed). -1pt. per pt. of energy stopped, -1 **END** per 50pt. of energy stopped, 1 Move.

ENERGY DRAIN/SURGE: (30**BP**, 3**BP**/1pt.) *Energy Drain* allows the Character to drain off the energy from a power source [not life] and release it harmlessly into the atmosphere (-30% to **CNC**, -50% in combat/rushed). -1pt. per 10pt. drained, -1 **END** per 25pt. drained, 1 Move per 25pt. drained. *Surge* is the reverse and can be used to overload systems.

ENERGY RETURN: (50**BP**, 5**BP**/1pt.) Permits a Character to return energy attacks to their source (-20% **CNC**, -40% combat/rushed). -1pt. per pt. energy, -1 **END** per 50pt. energy, 1 Move.

ENERGY SENSING: (20**BP**, 3**BP**/1pt.) Allows a Character to sense power sources [not life] (-20% **CNC**). -1pt. per 10' radius, -1 **END** per 10' radius, 1/2 Move per 10' radius.

LIGHT: (10**BP**, 2**BP**/1pt.) Allows the Character to illumine an area. The user seems to glow. -1pt. per 20' radius + -1 per round maintained, -1 **END** per round, 1/2 Move.

PSIONIC BLAST: (50**BP**, 5**BP**/1pt.) Allows the Character to focus a beam of destructive psionic energy at a target (-10% **CNC**). -1pt. per pt. of blast, -1 **END** per 2pt., 1/2 Move.

PYROKINETICS: (30**BP**, 3**BP**/1pt.) Allows a Character to raise the temperature of an object (-20% **CNC**, -40% **CNC** in combat/rushed). -1pt. per degree raised, -1 **END** per Move maintained, 1 Move.

TELEKINETIC SHIELD: (50**BP**, 2**BP**/1pt.) Allows the Character to form a barrier of psionic energy impervious to solids, liquids, or thick gases. Such a barrier may also be made airtight, but there is only 1 hour's worth of air per 10' diameter of sphere. Energy attacks using no material component cannot be stopped by the barrier (i.e., magical missiles, other psions, electricity). Plasma, flame (but not heat), and other attacks with a physical manifestation can be stopped (-10% to **CNC**, -30% if in combat or rushed). -1pt. per pt. of damage or object deflected + 1pt. per round held, - 2 **END** per round, 1 Move.

TELEKINETICS/LEVITATION: (50**BP**, 5**BP**/1pt.) Allows the Character to move objects with only his/her mind (-10% **CNC**, -30% in combat/rushed). -1pt. per 5 units + 1pt. per Phase, -1 **END** per 5 units, 1 Move. Levitation of oneself requires -25pts. + 1pt. per Phase + 1pt. per 10' of directional motion, -1 **END** per Phase, 1 Move.

THOUGHT SHIELD: (50**BP**, 5**BP**/1pt.) Similar to *Ward* except that this skill requires conscious use and stops magical attacks, Alterations, probes, or sensings as well (-30% **CNC**, -50% when in combat or rushed). -2pt. per pt. of magical attack warded, -1pt. per pt. of psion attack stopped, - 2 **END** per use against magic, -1 **END** per use against psion, 2 Moves.

WARD: (50**BP**, 3**BP**/1pt.) Forms a psionic barrier against psionic attacks, Alterations, probes, or sensings. Will automatically attempt activation whenever such psionic activities are directed at the Character (-10% **CNC**, -20% when in combat or rushed). -1pt. per pt. of psion stopped, -1 **END** per use, 1/2 Move.

Field of ALTERATIONS MATTER: (50**BP**, 5**BP**/1pt.) Allows a Character to buy psions within the Field of *Alterations Matter* as well as sense when such Alterations are being used (-20% **CNC**, -40% in combat/rushed). -1pt. per 10' radius, -1 **END** per 50' radius, 1 Move per 10' radius.

ANIMATE OBJECT: (50**BP**, 5**BP**/1pt.) Causes inanimate objects to move as the Character wills. Chairs may dance, tables may walk or take on some other semblance of life (-30% to **CNC**, -50% in combat/rushed). -5pts. per 20 units + -1pt. per Phase, -2 **END** + -1 **END** per Phase, 1 Move.

ASTRAL TRAVEL: (50**BP**, 5**BP**/1pt.) Allows the Psion to bring his/her body onto the Astral Plane. The Character cannot take equipment or other Characters along. However, he or she *can* move great distances rapidly (-30% to **CNC**, -50% in combat/rushed). -10pt. + -1pt. per mile, -1 **END** + -1 per mile, 1 Move per mile.

DETONATE: (50**BP**, 5**BP**/1pt.) Allows the Character to unleash the kinetic energy within an object forcefully, causing the object to explode. Does not work on living matter, but does work against animated organic materials like skeletons, wooden golems, and the like (-50% **CNC** in combat/rushed). -1pt. per pt. damage + -2 per 10', -1 **END** per use, 1 Move.

GREATER DETONATE: (100**BP**, 10**BP**/1pt.) This skill functions the same as *Detonate*, except that it works against living matter as well (-victim's **WILL**). -2pts. per 1pt. damage + -5pt. per 10', -5 **END** per use, 1 Move.

FOG: (30**BP**, 3**BP**/1pt.) Creates an area of dense fog around the user which allows only 1' of sight in any direction. It need not be water vapor; any substance that can vaporize naturally can be used. Just be aware that many vapors are poisonous (-10% in combat/rushed). -1pt. per 10' radius, -1 **END** per 50' radius, 1 Move per 50' radius.

QUAKE: (30**BP**, 5**BP**/1pt.) Allows the Character to cause vibrational tremors (-10% **CNC** in combat/rushed). -1pt. per pt. Richter + 1pt. per 10' radius, -2 **END** per 50' radius, 2 Moves.

TELEPORTATION: (100**BP**, 10**BP**/1pt.) Allows a Character to teleport to a known location. The teleporter must have actually seen or been to the spot before (if only astrally) or have received the image from another's mind (-50% **CNC**, -80% **CNC** in combat/rushed, + -10% per additional Character carried). -50pts. + -1pt. per mile + -1pt. per 10 units of additional weight carried, -10 **END** + -1pt. per mile + -1pt. per 50 units additional weight, 1 Move per mile.

WEATHER WORK: (50**BP**, 5**BP**/pt.) Permits a Character to alter weather in an area. If attempting to draw rain, the necessary moisture must be brought from some other location. The Character can sense weather patterns as well as alter them. This skill can only be used during combat to intensify or diminish a current weather pattern by one step. Character must *sense* first (-10% **CNC** to sense, -30% **CNC** to alter). -1pt. per mile to sense, -2pt. per mile to alter + -2pt. per round maintained, -1 **END** per mile sensed, -2 **END** per mile altered + -1 per round, 2 Moves per mile.

Field of ALTERATIONS PHYSICAL: (50**BP**) Allows the Character to buy psions within this Field as well as to sense the use of the listed psions in others (-10% **CNC**). -2pt. per use, -1 **END**, 1 Move. If used without touching as a *Sensing*, -5pt. per 10' radius, -1 **END** per 10' radius, 1 Move per 10' radius.

ASTRAL PROJECTION: (50**BP**, 2**BP**/1pt.) Allows the Character to separate the spirit or essence from the physical body and to travel great distances rapidly to see and hear what is happening elsewhere. A Character cannot be seen or heard except by those who can sense the Astral. There *are* dangers on the astral plane, however, as the physical body will be helpless while the spirit/essence is wandering (-20% **CNC**, -40% if in combat/rushed). -1pt. per mile plus 1pt. per round, -1 **END** per mile plus -1 **END** per round, 2 Moves.

FORCE ALTERATION: (100**BP**, 10**BP**/1pt.) Allows user to force one of the listed Alterations upon a victim (-70% to **CNC**, -90% if rushed). Forced alterations are permanent until undone.

Example: Ariel wants to Force Merge *Ruthgan into a pillar so he won't be spotted by searching Orcs. Merge costs 5pts. peruse, 2* **END**, *and 1 Move. To* Force Merge *will cost 10pts. peruse, 4* **END**, *and 2 Moves -- and if something happens to Ariel, poor Ruthgan will be stuck there until someone can* Force Merge *him back to normal.*
Add Alteration costs plus -5pt., -2 **END**, 1 Move.

MASK: (20**BP**, 3**BP**/1pt.) Allows the Psionic to change his/her facial features (-20% **CNC**, -30% in combat or if being followed). A specific face can be used if the Psionic has *Studied* the person before. -5pt. per round held, -2 **END** per round, 2 Moves.

MERGE: (20**BP**, 3**BP**/1pt.) Allows the Psionic to merge his/her body into any solid material. User cannot move while merged and cannot penetrate energy or force barriers (-20% to **CNC**, -30% in combat or if rushed). -5pt. per use, -2 **END**, 1 Move.

GREATER MERGE/PASS: (50**BP**, 5**BP**/1pt.) Allows user to move while merged. In this way the Character can pass through solids easily. Cannot pass force or energy barriers (-30% **CNC**, -50% if in combat or rushed). -10pt. per use, -5 **END**, 2 Moves.

METAMORPH: (50**BP**, 3**BP**/1pt.) Allows user to assume gaseous or liquid form (-50% **CNC**). -10pt. per use, -5 **END**, 2 Moves.

SHAPE SHIFT: (30**BP**, 3**BP**/1pt.) Allows the Character to alter his/her form. Does not change basic size or weight of Character, nor does it grant special powers. However, it *does* grant nonmagical characteristics of the form taken (i.e., heightened senses, strength, or speed). Includes inanimate objects. A specific form can be used if the Character has *Studied* the form before (-30% to **CNC**). -10pt. per round, -5 **END** per round, 4 Moves.

GREATER SHIFT: (50**BP**, 5**BP**/1pt.) Allows the user to alter his/her form with up to 50% size/weight increase or decrease. Does not grant any magical or psionic powers of the mimicked form. *Studied* forms may be used (-50% to **CNC**, -80% if rushed or in combat). -20pt. per round, -10 **END** per round, 8 Moves.

MASTER SHIFT: (100**BP**, 5**BP**/1pt) Allows total alteration of form without size or weight limitations. Does not grant any magical or psionic powers of the form taken. *Studied* forms may be used (-50% to **CNC**, -80% if rushed or in combat). -25pt. per round, -15 **END** per round, 12 Moves.

STUDY: (10**BP**, 3**BP**/1pt.) Allows the Character to memorize a face or form in such detail that it can be duplicated later with other psions. Gives a +10% **CNC** to Alterations which use *Study*. -1pt. per use, -1 **END**, 1 Move.

CIRCLE OF HEALING:

(50**BP**) Allows the Character to buy psions within the fields of **MIND HEALING**, **OTHERS HEALING**, and **SELF HEALING**. Character gains +10 **PSP** and 5% **CNC**. Evil Characters (**NPCs**) can buy the reverse of these psions: **MIND HARMING** and **OTHERS HARMING**. Player Characters do not normally have these as an option unless the **GM** allows, and even under such circumstances are required to learn them from a "master" of the evil arts.

Field of MIND HEALING: (50**BP**, 5**BP**/1pt.) Allows the Character to buy psions from within this Field, as well as to determine if someone's behavior is caused by trauma, imbalance, injury, or defect. A Character cannot heal his/her own mind. Curses cannot be cured with **MIND HEALING** (-30% to **CNC**, -50% if in combat, -60% if Character is a close friend or relative). -5pt. per use, -2 **END**, 4 Moves.

HEAL DEFECT: (50**BP**, 5**BP**/1pt.) Allows the Character to create new brain tissue or repair brain matter malfunctioning due to genetic defects(-50% to **CNC**). -25pt. per use, -15 **END**, 20 Moves.

HEAL IMBALANCE: (30**BP**, 3**BP**/1pt.) Allows a Character to heal mental disturbance caused by chemical imbalance or chemical dependency, by one step (see *Heal Trauma)*. This skill actually restores damaged tissues and causes a patient's brain to release the proper chemicals. -1/2 **WILL** of Character to be healed from the healer's **CNC**, as the chemical imbalance will prevent the ill Character from hindering or aiding the Psionic very much. -10pt. per step, -2 **END** per step, 4 Moves per step.

HEAL INJURY: (50**BP**, 5**BP**/1pt.) Allows the Character to heal damaged or lost brain tissue. Restores the brain to its normal state before the injury (-40% **CNC, -**50% if the Character is a close friend or relative). -20pt. per use, -10 **END**, 20 Moves.

HEAL TRAUMA: (30**BP**, 3**BP**/1pt.) Allows the Character to reduce trauma by one step (i.e., from *total* to *strong*, *strong* to *moderate*, *moderate* to *mild*, *mild* to *slim*, and *slim* to *none*). This can be used to remove *Psychological Limitations* caused by life experiences (**-WILL**% of Character to be healed from healer's **CNC,** because most Characters will resist mental tampering. Only 1/2 **WILL** penalty if the Character is cooperative). -5pt. per step, -1 **END** per step, 4 Moves per step.

RESTORE MEMORIES: (30**BP**, 3**BP**/1pt.) Allows the Psionic to restore memories lost due to mental tampering (-10% to **CNC** if in combat). -1pt. per pt. used in tampering, -2 **END**, 2 Moves. If simple amnesia or head blows caused memory loss, then -5pt. per use, -2 **END**, 2 Moves.

Field of OTHERS HEALING: (30**BP**, 3**BP**/1pt.) Allows a Character to buy psions within this Field, as well as to perform diagnosis on other Characters (-10% to **CNC**, -20% if in combat, -30% if the Character being healed is a friend or traveling companion, -50% if Character being healed is a loved one or close family member). -5pt. per use, -1 **END**, 1 Move. All **OTHERS HEALING** skills require the Psionic to physically touch the Character to be healed unless otherwise noted.

CLOSE WOUND: (20**BP**, 3**BP**/1pt.) Closes noncritical puncture wounds and cuts. -2pt. per use, -1 **END**, 1 Move.

GREATER CLOSING: (50**BP**, 5**BP**/1pt.) Closes critical cuts and puncture wounds. -15pt. per use, -10 **END**, 2 Moves.

CLOTTING: (10**BP**, 2**BP**/1pt.) Stops noncritical puncture wounds and cuts from bleeding. -2pt. per use, -1 **END**, 1 Move.

GREATER CLOTTING: (30**BP**, 3**BP**/1pt.) Stops critical puncture wounds and cuts from bleeding. -10pt. per use, -4 **END**, 2 Moves.

CURE DISEASE: (20**BP**, 3**BP**/1pt.) Cures bacterial and viral infections. -5pt. per use, -2 **END**, 2 Moves.

HEAL: (20**BP**, 3**BP**/1pt.) Restores lost blood and Hit Points to the Character up to 10pts. -2pt. per pt.healed, -3 **END**, 1 Move.

GREATER HEAL: (50**BP**, 5**BP**/1pt.) Restores lost blood and hit points to the Character. -2pt. per pt. healed, -5 **END** per 10pt. healed, 2 Moves.

MEND BONE: (30**BP**, 3**BP**/1pt.) Will heal broken bones or allow for the shaping of bone. -10pt. per use, -4 **END**, 2 Moves.

MEND FRACTURE: (10**BP**, 2**BP**/1pt.) Will heal bone fractures, but not breaks. -2pt. per use, -1 **END**, 1 Move.

NEUTRALIZE POISON: (30**BP**, 3**BP**/1pt.) Will neutralize a poisonous substance in the body. Does not make the Character immune to the substance. -5pt. per use, -2 **END**, 2 Moves.

PAIN RELIEF: (10**BP**, 2**BP**/1pt.) Stops the Character from feeling pain. **CNC** penalties are reduced by 1/2. -1pt. per use, -1 **END**, 1 Move.

PARALYZE: (30**BP**, 3**BP**/1pt.) Makes the victim unable to move or thrash about. -1pt. per Move paralyzed, -1 **END** per 4 Moves paralyzed, 1 Move.

PSYCHIC SURGERY: (50**BP**, 5**BP**/1pt.) Allows the Character to remove tumors, parts of weapons which have broken off, or other damaging materials from within a victim's body without leaving or enlarging wounds (-30% to **CNC**, -60% if Character is a friend or loved one). -10pt. per use, -5 **END**, 3 Moves.

REGENERATE: (50**BP**, 5**BP**/1pt.) Allows the Character to regenerate lost limbs or injured organs if the wound is not immediately fatal. Will not restore brain tissue or heal nerve damage. Character will go into a trance state. -50pt. per use, -15 **END**, 20 Moves.

RESTORE NERVES: (30**BP**, 5**BP**/1pt.) Heals or regenerates damaged or lost nerve tissue. Will not repair brain tissues (see *Mind Healing*). Can cure paralysis and spinal injuries. -15pt. per use, -8 **END**, 4 Moves.

SLEEP: (30**BP**, 3**BP**/1pt.) Causes the victim to go to sleep. Character will sleep until disturbed. -5pt. per round sleep, -2 **END** per round sleep, 1 Move.

TISSUE REPAIR: (10**BP**, 3**BP**/1pt.) Repairs torn muscles or tendons. -2pt. per use, -1 **END**, 1 Move.

Field of SELF-HEALING: (30**BP**, 3**BP**/1pt.) Allows the Character to buy healing psions within this Field. Also allows the Character to perform self-diagnosis. Costs 5pt. per use (-20% to **CNC** if injury is minor, -50% to **CNC** if injury is major, -80% to **CNC** if critical, to all use of psions in this field). -1 **END**, 2 Moves.

CLOSE WOUND: (20**BP**, 3**BP**/1pt.) Closes noncritical puncture wounds and cuts. -1pt. per use, -1 **END** per use,1 Move.

GREATER CLOSING: (50**BP**, 5**BP**/1pt.) Closes critical cuts and puncture wounds. -10pt. per use, -5 **END**, 2 Moves.

CLOTTING: (10**BP**, 2**BP**/1pt.) Stops noncritical puncture wounds and cuts from bleeding. -1pt. per use, -1 **END** per use, 1 Move.

GREATER CLOTTING: (30**BP**, 3**BP**/1pt.) Stops critical puncture wounds and cuts from bleeding. -5pt. per use, -2 **END**, 2 Moves.

CURE DISEASE: (20**BP**, 3**BP**/1pt.) Cures bacterial and viral infections. -2pt. per use, -1 **END**, 1 Move.

HEAL: (20**BP**, 3**BP**/1pt.) Restores lost blood and Hit Points to the Psionic up to 10pts. -1pt. per pt. healed, -2 **END** per use, 1 Move.

GREATER HEAL: (50**BP**, 5**BP**/1pt.) Restores lost blood and hit points to the Psionic. -1pt. per pt. healed, -2 **END** per 10pt. healed, 2 Moves.

MEND BONE: (30**BP**, 3**BP**/1pt.) Will heal broken bones or allow for the shaping of bone. -5pt. per use, -2 **END**, 1 Move.

MEND FRACTURE: (10**BP**, 2**BP**/1pt.) Will heal bone fractures, but not breaks. -1pt., -1 **END**, 1 Move.

NEUTRALIZE POISON: (30**BP**, 3**BP**/1pt.) Will neutralize a poisonous substance in the Psionic's body. Does not, however, make the Character immune to the substance. This psion will automatically try to kick in if the Psionic is poisoned. -5pt. per use, -1 **END**, 1 Move.

PAIN RELIEF: (10**BP**, 2**BP**/1pt.) Stops the Psionic from feeling pain. **CNC** penalties are reduced by 1/2. -1pt. per use, -1 **END**, 1 Move.

REGENERATE: (50**BP**, 5**BP**/1pt.) Allows the Psionic to regenerate lost limbs or injured organs as long as the wound is not instantly fatal. Will not restore brain tissue or heal nerve damage. Psionic will go into a trance state. This psion will automatically attempt to kick in when needed. -20pt. per use, -10 **END**, 20 Moves.

RESTORE NERVES: (30**BP**, 5**BP**/1pt.) Heals or regenerates damaged or lost nerve tissue. Will not repair brain tissues (see *Mind Healing*). Can cure paralysis and spinal injuries. -10pt. per use, -5 **END**, 4 Moves.

TISSUE REPAIR: (10**BP**, 3**BP**/1pt.) Repairs torn muscles or tendons. -1pt. per use, -1 **END**, 1 Move.

CIRCLE OF THE MIND:

(50**BP**) Allows a Character to buy psions in the Fields of **MIND COMMUNICATION/ATTACK, MIND DEFENSE/ ILLUSIONS,** and **MIND VISIONS/SENSINGS**. Gives 10 **PSP** and +5% **CNC**.

Field of MIND COMMUNICATION/ATTACK: (50**BP**, 3**BP**/1pt.) Allows a Character to buy psions within the Field of *Mind Communication/Attack* as well as to detect the use of such psions (-10% **CNC**). -1pt. per 10' sensing, -1 **END** per 50' sensing, 1 Move per 50'.

ADJUST MEMORIES: (30**BP**, 3**BP**/1pt.) Allows the Character to reconstruct a single set of memories (-1/2 **WILL** of victim to **CNC**). Requires Psionic to physically touch the victim. -5pt. per set of memories altered, -2 **END**, 2 Moves per set of memories.

ANIMAL CONTROL: (30**BP**, 3**BP**/1pt.) Allows a Character to control the actions of animals (**INT** of 8 or lower). The animal's normal **MA** and **AG** are reduced to 1/2, and the animal takes -1 **END** per Phase (-**WILL** of animal to **CNC**). -5pt. + -2pt. per Phase + -1 per 10', -1 **END** per Phase, 1 Move.

CHOKE: (30**BP**, 5**BP**/1pt.) Allows the Psionic to cause choking within a victim. (1/2 **CON** = number of Phases victim will remain conscious. **CON** = number of Phases before death). This ability can be used from a distance (-**WILL** of victim to **CNC**). -10pt. per victim + -1 per Phase + -1 per 10', -2 **END** per round, 1 Move.

DATA ALTER: (10**BP**, 5**BP**/1pt.) Allows a Character to change information in a file. Character must be able to *Interface* first (-20% to **CNC**). -5pt. per alteration, -2 **END**, 1 Move per alteration.

DATA SWIPE: (10**BP**, 3**BP**/1pt.) Allows the Character to memorize a file. Character must be able to *Interface* first (-20% to **CNC**). -5pt. per file, -2 **END**, 2 Moves.

DATA WIPE: (20**BP**, 5**BP**/1pt.) Allows the Character to erase a file. Character must be able to *Interface* first (-40% to **CNC**). -10pt. per file, -5 **END**, 2 Moves.

DETECT LIE: (10**BP**, 2**BP**/1pt.) Allows a Character to know when someone is lying. -2pt. + -1pt. per round + -1pt. per 10' radius, -1 **END** per round, 1 Move.

EMPATHIC BOND: (30**BP**, 5**BP**/1pt.) Establishes a permanent link to another Character. The Psionic will always be able to tap into this link in order to feel emotions or sensations from the other Character. The link must be actively blocked to avoid these sensations. *Empathic Bond* also allows the Psionic to gain information from the other Character's senses: to see what he/she sees, hear what he/she hears, etc. If the Bonded Character is injured while this link is open, the Psionist will take 1/2 the damage from *mind trauma*. A link is always considered open unless one of the Characters states he/she is blocking and spends the points to do so. However, a Character must have psionic abilities in order to break the bond (-2pt. per link to block + -1pt. per Phase, -2 **END** per round, 1/2 Move). -2pt. per link to set, -1 **END** per link to set, 2 Moves to set.

EMPATHY: (30**BP**, 3**BP**/1pt.) Allows a Character to feel emotions and physical sensations from another. The Character must be in physical contact with the other unless an empathic bond has been established (-1/2 **WILL** of victim to **CNC** if resisting). -5pt. per use, -2 **END**, 2 Moves.

INTERFACE/PARATRONICS: (30**BP**, 5**BP**/1pt.) Allows a Character to mentally link with a computer or other electronic systems. Allows the Character to access and read files, travel through information networks and ride carrier signals. (-50% to **CNC**, -80% if in combat/rushed) Character is unaware of his or her physical body while in *Interface*. -2pt. to link + -1 for each file accessed or read, or each net link up passed. -1 **END** per phase spent in interface, 1 Move to link + 1 Move per file read or accessed, or each net link passed.

LANGUAGE SWIPE: (40**BP**, 3**BP**/1pt.) Allows the user to learn a language from the victim's mind at the same level of skill (-1/2 victim's **WILL** to **CNC**, -30% if victim is cooperating). -20pt. per use, -6 **END**, 8 Moves.

MEMORY SWIPE: (30**BP**, 3**BP**/1pt.) Allows the Character to copy into his or her own mind one set of memories (-1/2 **WILL** of victim to **CNC**). -5pt. per set of memories, -2 **END**, 2 Moves per set of memories.

MIND CONTROL: (50**BP**, 5**BP**/1pt.) Allows a Character to control the actions of creatures (**INT** of 8 or higher). The creature's normal **MA** and **AG** are reduced to 1/2, and the victim suffers -1 **END** per Phase (-**WILL** of victim to **CNC**). -10pt. + -2pt. per Phase + -1pt. per 10', -5 **END** per Phase, 1 Move.

MIND MELD: (50**BP**, 3**BP**/1pt.) Allows two or more Psionics to pool their **PSP** and channel it through another ability. The Character controllng the Meld cannot use other psions while maintaining the Meld, although the other Psionics may. All Characters involved will take full **END** loss for all actions. **PSP** loss, however, is divided among the Characters (-20% to **CNC**, -30% in combat/rushed, +-10% for each Psionic Melded after the first two, the Melder and the first Character Melded being the first two). Requires all Characters Melded to be in physical contact with each other. -5pt. per Psionic, -2 **END** per Psionic per Phase, 1 Move per Psionic.

MIND SCAN: (20**BP**, 3**BP**/1pt.) Allows the Character to scan the surface thoughts of another creature. -2pt. per use + -1 per 100', -1 **END**, 1 Move.

MIND-TO-MIND/TELEPATHY: (10**BP**, 3**BP**/1pt.) Allows the Character to send a specific thought, word, or image to another Character or creature (**INT** of 8 or more). Only Characters with *Mind-to-Mind* can send responses back. Requires the Characters to have physically touched previously. -1pt. per word or image, -1 **END** per 10 words or images, 1 Move per mile.

MIND WIPE: (50**BP**, 5**BP**/1pt.) Allows the Character to wipe a victim's mind clean (-**WILL** of victim from **CNC**). A successful attack will leave the victim in an infantile mental state. -25pt. per use, -10 **END**, 8 Moves.

PAIN: (20**BP**, 3**BP**/1pt.) Allows the Psionic to cause intense pain in others. Such an attack reduces **WILL** and **CNC** of the victim by 1/2. All victim's skills will be at -50% as long as the *Pain* lasts (-30% to **CNC**). -10pt. per victim + -1pt. per Move maintained, -2 **END** per victim + -1 per Phase, 1 Move.

PROBE: (30**BP**, 3**BP**/1pt.) Allows a Character to search a victim's mind in order to find a specific thought or skill. Without this ability, the Psionic must search at random in the victim's mind (-1/2 victims **WILL** to **CNC**). -10pt. per probe, -4 **END**, 1 Phase.

RAPPORT: (10**BP**, 3**BP**/1pt.) Allows the Character to communicate with creatures (**INT** of 8 or less) through images and emotions. This skill permits communication only, not control. -5pt. per use, -1 **END**, 1 Move.

UNLEARN: (50**BP**, 5**BP**/1pt.) Allows the user to make a Character forget one skill. Must start with highest level of skill. Requires physical contact.

Example: A Character must remove the victim's Dagger 3 *skill, then* Dagger 2 *skill before he or she can eliminate the* Dagger *skill. All* Blade *skills must be removed before the victim's* Blade *class skill can be removed, etc.*(-1/2 **WILL** of victim to **CNC**). -25pt. per skill, -5 **END**, 2 Moves.

Field of MIND DEFENSE/ILLUSION: (50**BP**, 3**BP**/1pt.) Allows the Character to buy psions in the field of *Mind Defense/Illusion*. Some of these psions cannot be detected: *Cloak Mind, Cloak Pattern, Mind Fortress, and Sensing Shield*. All others can be detected.

CHAMELEON: (30**BP**, 3**BP**/1pt.) Causes the user and his/her equipment to take on the pattern of whatever they are near. This will give searchers a -80% probability of seeing them, even affecting the heat signature so that *Infravision* is fooled. In actuality, this psion affects the eyes of the viewer and not the user or the equipment, but this isn't widely believed. -5pt. per use + -1pt. per round, -1 **END** per round, 1 Move.

CLOAK AURA: (30**BP**, 5**BP**/1pt.) Hides the Psionic's aura from *Aura Vision* so that an *Aura Lock* cannot be made. -10pt. per use, -1 **END** per use, 1/2 Move.

CLOAK PATTERN: (20**BP**, 3**BP**/1pt.) Blocks an item's energy pattern so that it cannot be *Sensed* or *Studied* psionically. Item must be physically touched to initiate. (-10% to **CNC**) -5pt. per object, -1 **END** per object, 1 Move per object.

ILLUSION: (100**BP**, 5**BP**/1pt.) Draws an image from the Psionic's or the victim's mind and makes it visible to everyone in the area of effect. To those not targeted, the images appear ghostlike. To those targeted, the image looks, feels, smells, sounds, and even tastes real. It is even possible to kill with such an illusion. The illusion is always under the control of the Psionic. This skill has a 60' radius effect. Each Phase, the victim may make a **WILL** roll to resist. Each failed roll adds a -10% penalty to the next roll, and these are cumulative (-**WILL** of victim to **CNC**. Each target requires a separate roll). -50pt. + -2pt. per Phase, -2 **END** per Phase, 3 Moves.

INVISIBILITY: (50**BP**, 5**BP**/1pt.) Like *Chameleon,* this ability actually affects the senses of others rather than those of the Psionic. The Character will be hidden from sight or hearing so long as loud noises aren't made (anything louder than breathing is considered a loud noise when dealing with superior hearing). -10pt. per use + -1 per round, -1 **END** per round, 2 Moves.

MIND FORTRESS: (100**BP**, 10**BP**/1pt.) Draws on the latent psionic talents in all sentient beings to form a psionic barrier. No Character in physical contact with the user can be directly attacked or detected by the use of any psion. Uses all protected Character's pooled **PSP** to deflect psions, 1pt. per pt., after which the barrier will fall. Once set, Fortressed Characters may move away from the Psionic who built the fortress--up to a distance of 60' away--and still receive protection (-10% to **CNC** per Character shielded). -25pt. per Character shielded + -1 per Character each round, -1 **END** per Character + -1 **END** per Character each round, 2 Moves.

OVERLOOK: (20**BP**, 3**BP**/1pt.) If nothing is done to attract attention, this skill causes the victim to simply ignore the user. This is an area effect, and all Characters the Psionic doesn't want noticed can also be *Overlooked* (-10% to **CNC**, -30% in combat/rushed, + -10% per Character). -5pt. per Character + -1 per 10' radius, -1 **END** per round + -1 per Character, 2 Moves.

PSION SHIELD: (50**BP**, 5**BP**/1pt.) This skill creates a personal psion barrier around the user, blocking all psions helpful or harmful. This lasts until the user either runs out of power to maintain it or voluntarily lets it down. -10pt. + -1pt. per round + -1pt. per pt. of psion blocked, -1 **END** per round, 1/2 Move.

SENSING SHIELD: (30**BP**, 5**BP**/1pt.) Creates an area where no *Sensings* or *Far Seeings* will work, or hides the user from *Sensings* or *Far Seeing* (-30% to **CNC** for area, -10% to **CNC** for self). -10pt. per 60' radius + -1 per round, -1 **END** per round, 2 Moves or -5pt. + -1 per round, -1 **END** per round, 1 Move.

SUGGESTION: (30**BP**, 5**BP**/1pt.) Allows the Psionic to give a spoken suggestion to a victim. This skill can't be used to make a victim do harm to him- or herself (-1/2 **WILL** victim to **CNC**). -2pt. per suggestion, -1 **END** per use, 2 Moves.

Field of MIND VISIONS/SENSING: (50**BP**, 3**BP**/1pt.) Allows the Character to buy psions in the Field of *Mind Visions/Sensing*, as well as to detect the use of such psions (-10% to **CNC**,-30% in combat/ rushed). -2pt. per use + 1pt. per 20' radius, -1 **END** per 100',1 Move per 20'.

AURA LOCK/TRACK: (30**BP**, 5**BP**/1pt.) Lets the Character memorize a living thing's aura patterns and track it by following the energy trail. A pattern will hold for 1 week per hour spent in a location, and just passing through an area leaves a trace which lasts 24 hours. A Character must have Aura Vision before using this psion (-20% **CNC**, -50% in combat/ rushed). -10pt. per lock, -1 **END** per lock, 1 Move per lock, -2pt. per 1 mile to track, -1 **END** per round to track, 1/2 Move to start track.

AURA VISION: (30**BP**, 5**BP**/1pt.) Lets the user see the energy pattern of living things. It will give a reading of current emotions, show if a person is cursed or has been mentally tampered with. However, since living things tend to change from good to evil according to situation and Character viewpoint, this cannot be determined by *Aura Vision*. Target Character must be in clear visual range (-40% to **CNC**, -70% in combat/rushed). -10pt. per aura, -2 **END** per aura, 1 Move per aura.

DANGER SENSE: (50**BP**, 5**BP**/1pt.) This ability is subconscious and always active. It gives the Character a slowly increasing warning buzz or tingling in his/her mind. Actual sensing can give the Character a more specific idea of how soon (immediate, near future, far future), where (immediate, near, far, distant), or what kind of danger (physical, mental, essence/ spirit) is imminent (-50% to **CNC**). -10pt. per sensing(when, where, what), -1 **END** per sensing, 1/2 Move per sensing.

DETECT PSIONS: (30**BP**, 3**BP**/1pt.) Allows a Character to detect psions being used or to pick up traces of psion use. Psion traces last up to three weeks in an area before fading completely. The Character will be able to tell how far in the past the psion was used. Mind Defense psions which can't be *Detected* will read as unknown energy, as will magic, energy beings, and other such things (-10% per day to **CNC** for traces). -5pt. per 10' radius, -1 **END** per 10' radius, 1 Move per 10' radius.

FAR LISTENING: (50**BP**, 5**BP**/1pt.) Allows the Character to hear what is happening in a place he/she has never been before. The Character must have been in the place physically for one day or more in order to *Far Listen* it and cannot listen to places from within others' minds. This skill also allows a Character to hear anything within the immediate surroundings (up to 20 square feet) about an item he/she has *Pattern Studied* or about a person he/she has *Aura Locked*. *Far Seeing* and *Far Listening* can be used in conjuction with each other (-50% to **CNC**, -80% in combat/ rushed). -10pt. per place + -1pt. per mile distant, -2 **END** + -1pt. per 20 miles distant, 1 Move per 20 miles distant.

FAR SEEING: (50**BP**, 5**BP**/1pt.) Allows the Character to see what is happening in a place he/she has never been before. The Psionic must have been in the place physically for one day or more in order to *Far See* it. The Character cannot listen to places from within others' minds. This skill also allows a Character to see anything within the immediate surroundings (up to 20 square feet) about an item he/she has *Pattern Studied* or about a person he/she has *Aura Locked*. *Far Seeing* and *Far Listening* can be used in conjuction with each other (-50% to **CNC**, -80% in combat/ rushed). -10pt. per place + -1pt. per mile distant, -2 **END** + -1pt. per 20 miles distant, 1 Move per 20 miles distant.

IDENTIFY PSIONS: (30**BP**, 3**BP**/1pt.) Allows a Character to know which psion is being used against him or her. If the user can *Detect Psion*, he or she can identify not only what psions are currently in use, but psion traces as well. A Mind Defense psion which can't be *Identified* will be considered an unknown psion. -5pt. per use, -1 **END**, 1/2 Move. On detect: -5pt. per 10' radius, -1 **END** per 10' radius, 1 Move per 10' radius.

ITEM'S FUTURE: (20**BP**, 5**BP**/1pt.) Allows a Character to glimpse an event in an object's future. Sometimes the image received is symbolic rather than actual (-30% to **CNC**, -60% in combat/rushed). -10pt. per image, -1 **END** per image, 1 Move per image.

ITEM'S PAST: (30**BP**, 5**BP**/1pt.) Allows a Character to glimpse an event which happened in an object's past. These events are rarely symbolic (-30% to **CNC**, -60% in combat/rushed). -10pt. per image, -1 **END** per image, 1 Move per image.

PATTERN STUDY: (50**BP**, 3**BP**/1pt.) This ability allows the Character to memorize and analyze the energy pattern of an object. It gives a general impression of whether the thing is good, evil, or neutral. Will also show if an object is cursed or sentient (-20% to **CNC**, -50% in combat/rushed). -10pt. per object, -2 **END**, 2 Moves.

PRECOGNITION: (50**BP**, 5**BP**/1pt.) [*Note to the* **GM**-- *You'll have to plan ahead on this one.*] Allows the Character brief glimpses of the future. These images are sometimes symbolic rather than actual, but they always come true (-50% to **CNC**). -10pt. per image, -2 **END**, 4 Moves.

PRESENCE SENSE: (50**BP**, 5**BP**/1pt.) This ability locates sentient minds (**INT** 8 or higher) in a given area. Works in a fashion similar to *Sense Life* except that it filters out all creatures with **INT** less than 8 (-20% to **CNC**, -50% if in combat/rushed). -5pt. per 20', -2 **END** per 50', 1 Move per 20'.

RETROCOGNITION: (50**BP**, 5**BP**/1pt.) Allows the Character brief glimpses into the past. These images are rarely symbolic and are always accurate (-50% to **CNC**). -10pt. per image, -2 **END**, 4 Moves.

SENSE LIFE: (30**BP**, 5**BP**/1pt.) Allows the Character to be aware of all life forms and their general distance and direction from the user (-10% to **CNC**, -30% if in combat/rushed). -2pt. per 10'radius, -1 **END** per 50', 1/2 Move per 10'.

Magic

There are several forms of magic in the **Webs Gaming System**.

Spells are given in the game supplements and vary from game to game. Some forms of magic may not be available in certain campaigns, so check with your **GM** before choosing magic. All power is recovered at 1pt. per round when spell casting.

All spells in the **Webs** System use the following format:

- **Name**: The name of the spell
- **Limitations**: Atrributes needed to use the spell
- **Will**: Bonuses or penalties to **WILL** when casting the spell
- **CNC**: Bonuses or penalties to **CNC** when casting the spell
- **Saving Roll**: What a victim must do to save him or herself from the effects of the spell
- **Casting Time**: How long it takes to cast the spell
- **Duration**: How long the effect lasts
- **Range**: Area of effect
- **Cost**: How much power is needed for the spell
- **Type**: Whether the spell *is Clerical*, *Manate*, *Essence/Spirit*, or *Ritual*
- **Effect**: What the spell does
- **Equipment**: Materials needed to cast which are not used up in the process
- **Expendables**: Materials needed to cast which are used up in the process
- **Ceremony**: Necessary words or motions normally needed to cast
- **Misfire**: What happens if you fail
- **Memorize**: How long it takes to rememorize the spell
- **Counter**: Spells most often used against the spell cast

Since all Clerics have *Sanctify* and *Create Holy/Unholy Water* which have the same effect (*Blessing* may have different effects from deity to deity), I will use them as examples:

Name: **Create Holy/Unholy Water**
Limitations: None
WILL: +10% unless in combat
CNC: +10% unless in combat
Saving Roll: None
Casting Time: 1 Move per ounce
Duration: Permanent
Range:10'
Cost: 1pt. per ounce
Type: Clerical
Effect: Creates holy or unholy water, depending on the alignment of the deity served.
Equipment: A container for the water
Expendables: None
Ceremony: Caster need only call for the deity's assistance and then touch or motion toward the container.
Misfire: Results in no water and lost points.
Memorize:10 Moves
Counter: *Break Spell*, *Curse/Bless Water*

Name: **Sanctify**
Limitations: None
WILL: +20% unless in combat
CNC: +20% unless in combat
Saving Roll: None
Casting time: 5 Moves
Duration: Permanent
Range: Special
Cost: 1pt. per 10' radius
Type: Clerical
Effect: Creates an area of holy/unholy ground for a particular deity so that altars, temples, graveyards, etc., may be established.
Equipment: None
Expendables: 1oz. holy/unholy water
Ceremony: Caster sprinkles the water onto the area and calls upon his/her deity to bless it.
Misfire: Results in loss of points with no effect.
Memorize: 5 Moves
Counter: *Curse/Bless Land*

Due to the nature of magic Characters can only memorize their **INT** worth of spells for a day. Once they use that spell from memory, it becomes flawed and cannot be used again until rememorized.

Types of Magic

Clerical Magic is granted by the Celestial Powers of the Deities. Deities have limited spheres of influence and have little to no power where they have no followers. The advantages are that spells are granted by the Deity and will not need to be found; the spells are cast by faith and do not need components; and the Deity may sometimes intervene to save a favored Cleric.

Manate Magic takes *"mana"* from objects to power spells. Since the power is taken from outside sources, the caster rarely uses up his or her personal reserves. It is, however, necessary that this type of **Spellcaster** carry large amounts of mana-charged items.

Essence/Spirit Magic draws on the personal power of the **Spellcaster**. This allows the caster to perform spells with no need to carry components but increases the risk of *spellburn*.

Ritual Magic uses elaborate ceremonies to create power. It requires certain actions to be performed at specific times and in specific ways. This is a slow form of magic, but its effects are often more powerful than those of other magics.

Note: *A **Spellcaster** may know how to use more than one type of magic, but Clerics are often limited to only one type or are forbidden certain kinds by their Deity. Check with your **GM** before using more than one kind of magic.*

In order to cast spells, a form of magic must be chosen and certain skills must be bought. These skills are:

SPELLCASTER:(100**BP**) Allows the Character to *Read/Write* and *Speak Magic* at 90 +/-**PA** bonus/penalty (3**BP**/1pt.). Character knows the formula for magic ink. This skill is not needed by Clerics.

COMMUNION:(50**BP**) Allows the Character to tap into and focus the energies given to him or her by a Deity. All Clerics have a *Blessing, Sanctify*, and *Create Holy/Unholy Water* spell. They will also have a holy/unholy symbol. *Communion* is needed only by Clerics.

ESSENCE/SPIRIT CAST: (50**BP**) Allows the caster to tap his/her own personal power to cast spells.

MANA CAST:(50**BP**) Allows the caster to tap into the **mana** stored in objects. Without this skill a Character cannot use mana for spellcasting.

RITUAL CAST: (50**BP**) Allows the caster to draw power from rituals to cast spells.

Spellmasters

The **Spellmaster** is a special form of spellcaster. This Character has chosen magic for the focus of his or her life and can therefore not use *psions* which tap into other forms of energy, nor can they become **Weaponmasters** who devote their time to the practice of weapon use. In return for this sacrifice, they are given access to skills to which other Characters are not allowed access. A Character may not change his or her mind later; once the **Spellmaster** path is chosen, **Weaponmastery** or **Psimastery** skills cannot be learned.

CARVE FETISH: (100**BP**, 3**BP**/1pt.) This skill starts at Base 50% and must be bought up. It allows the caster to carve bone, stone, or wooden fetishes in such a way that they have more **mana** than normal. There is a -2% on this skill per 1pt. **mana** desired to successfully carve a fetish.

*Example: Raven has a wolf tooth. It only has 1 **mana** point (3 if used for* Hunting/Tracking *spells,* Hearing Spells, *or* Animal Charming*). She wants to carve it to add +9 **mana**. 9x2=18 so she has her skill% - 18 to carve it. Her skill is 50% - 18 = 32% to carve the fetish. It takes 1 Phase per pt. to carve fetishes, so it will take her 9 Phases, or 36 Moves.*

She sits down to carve and rolls a 28. She should be able to carve the fetish if nothing disturbs her.

Say she only gets to Move 15, and then is interrupted by a call for help. She will have to roll again to see if her next carving session is successful. If so, she can complete her fetish.

*If she fails a roll after an initial success, then the carving is flawed. There will be an increase in **mana** -- just not as much as she'd desired. The **GM** must decide in a case like this how much less. If the first roll of an attempt is failed, then there is no increase in **mana**, and a possible loss of **mana** points. Once again, the **GM** must decide, based on by how much the roll was missed.*

ESSENCE/SPIRIT BOOST: (50**BP**) Allows a caster to buy power points *Beyond Racial Maximum* **(BRM)** with 10**BP** per 1pt. For every 100pts. purchased there is a +10% chance of *spellburn*.

QUICK CAST: (100**BP**) Reduces casting time for the Character by 1/2.

MANA SENSE: (30**BP**, 5**BP**/1pt.) Allows a Character to sense **mana** webs and nodes, and get an idea of how much **mana** can be pulled from them. This Character can also tell how much **mana** is in an object (5pt. per use + 1pt. per 10'). Requires 1 Move.

MANA TAP: (100**BP**, 10**BP**/1pt.) Allows the **Spellcaster** to tap into **mana** webs and nodes to power spells. All worlds which support life have **mana** webs and nodes -- even some planets *without* life have them. The caster can pull 1pt. of **mana** per 5pt. of *Mana Tap* used to add to their spells. Requires 1 Move.

MEMORY BOOST: (10**BP**) Allows the Character to increase the number of spells he/she can memorize for a day by 1 per time taken.

SENSE MAGIC: (20**BP**, 3**BP**/1pt.) Allows Characters who do not have this ability naturally to sense if items are magical or to sense if magic is being used. The ability will automatically kick in if a player is magically attacked 1/2 Move before the spell hits. 1pt. per warning, 5pts. per use + 1pt. per 20' radius. Requires 1 Move per 20'.

SPELL MEMORY: (100**BP**) Allows the Character to double the amount of spells he or she can memorize for a day. Can only be taken once.

SPELL STACKING: (50**BP**, 5**BP**/1pt.) Lets the Character stack spells of a related nature to perform a specific effect (for example, stacking a *Daggers of Ice* and a *Daggers of Flame* spell so that both fire and ice daggers are created. Adding *Dazzle* spell would give the victims penalties to dodge). The casting times are added together but the spells go off simultaneously (10pts. per spell stacked).

SPELL STORING: (50**BP**, 10**BP**/1pt.) Allows a Character to precast spells into a "magical ether space" which will go off when the caster performs a predetermined trigger (action, word, etc., which must be specified). The Character can store as many spells as he or she has spell storing skill to handle. (A 25pt. *Fireball* takes 25pts. to store, so at Base level a Character could only store two of them, and must release one of them before something else can be stored). Casting times of spells are added.

SPELL STYLING: (30**BP**) Allows a Character to change how a spell is performed or cast to better suit his/her style. Character must specify styling format (Hand Gestures, Command Words, Songs, Rhymes, Riddles, Symbols, Items, etc.). Each manner of styling must be purchased separately. Each spell styled and how it is styled must be cleared by the **GM** before use in play (costs 10pts. per change made to a spell. The new spell is recorded in the Character's spell book and can be used in the same way again).

Example: Raven has the spell Daggers of Flame. *She normally needs a handful of sand to cast the spell, but decides that this takes up too much room in her pouches, so she wants to be able to cast the spell without using sand. She decides to use a command word instead:* "flambe." *So she spends 10* Buy Points *from her* ***"buy pool"*** *to purchase the altered version of the spell. It costs her 10pt. for every change she makes to any spell, and she must clear each change with the* **GM**.

Weaponmasters

The **Weaponmaster** has devoted his or her life to the art of weapon play. Like the **Spellmaster,** the **Weaponmaster** must stay on the path he/she has chosen. The Character can never learn **Spellmaster**, or **Psimaster** skills. This does not mean that he or she cannot use psions or spells, but that this is the only class able to use **Weaponmaster** skills.

ARMOR USE: (20**BP**) Allows the Character to increase his/her effective **AC** by 1 per time taken to a maximum of +5**AC** due to the skill and ease which comes from always wearing the armor.

DEATH FRENZY: (10**BP**) Allows the Character to stay standing in combat and fight on for 1phase per time taken, even when fatally wounded -- until head is severed or until arms and legs have been removed. Not much help to the Character, but it could save his or her friends.

FURY: (20**BP**) Allows the Character to halve **END** costs when fighting, losing only 1pt. per Phase rather than the usual 2.

Fury 2: Allows loss of 1pt. per 2 Phases
Fury 3: 1pt. per 3 Phases
Fury 4: 1pt. per 4 Phases
Fury 5: 1pt. per 5 Phases.

Note: Fury 5 is the highest level of this skill allowed.

WAR CRY: (10**BP**) Reduces all opponents' weapon skills by 5% per time taken, as well and boosts all comrades' weapons skills by 5% per time taken.

WEAPON MASTERY: (30**BP**/weapon class) Allows the Character to buy up to *Weapon Skill 6* with weapons in a specific class.

Psimasters

These Characters have devoted their lives to unlocking the secrets of the mind. Once this choice is made, the Character can never learn **Weaponmastery** or **Spellmastery**. **Psimasters** can't use magic, because their bodies are tuned to a different form of energy, but they *can use* magical items.

ASTRAL RESTORE: (50**BP**, 10**BP**/1pt.) Allows the Character to restore lost **PSP** and **END** by tapping into the Astral web and nodes. Costs 5pts. per 1pt. restored. *Astral Tap* is required. Requires 4 Moves.

ASTRAL SENSE: (30**BP**, 5**BP**/1pt.) Ability to sense the astral web streams and nodes. Gives Character an idea of how much power can be drawn from them. 5pts. per use + 1pt. per 10'. Requires 1 Move.

ASTRAL TAP: (100**BP**, 10**BP**/1pt.) Allows the Character to tap into the astral web and nodes. The Character can draw 1pt. of **PSP** per 5 pts. of *Tap* to use in psions. A web stream or node must be present to use this skill. Requires 1 Move.

PSIBOOST: (50**BP,** 10**BP/**1pt.) Allows the Character to buy **PSP** beyond Racial maximums at 10**BP/**1pt. Every 100pts. above Racial maximum increases psiburn chances by +10%.

PSI STACKING: (50**BP**, 5**BP/**1pt.) Allows use of more than one psion simulataneously. 10pts. per psion stacked plus -1 **END** per 2 psions. Movement costs are added.

Physical Adepts

Physical Adept skills are a cross between extreme physical training, psion discipline, supernatural force, and scientific mutation.

Physical Adept skills defy clear-cut classification but are available to anyone who is able to find a teacher.

AIRWALK: (20**BP**, 5**BP/**1pt.) Ability to walk on air. 1pt. per 10'.

ASTRAL HEARING: (20**BP**, 3**BP/**1pt.) Lets the Character hear what is happening on the astral plane. The sound will be distorted (echo- or static-filled but understandable). 1pt. per 10'.

ASTRAL VISION: (20**BP**, 3**BP/**1pt.) This ability lets the user see onto the astral plane. This vision can not be used with other visions. 1pt. per 10'.

ASTRAL VOICE: (20**BP**, 3**BP/**1pt.) Allows a Character to speak to those on the astral plane without being heard on the Prime Material Plane (that's what we live on). 1pt. per word.

CHAKRA SCREAM: (50**BP**, 5**BP/**1pt.) Allows the Character to disrupt a "chakra point" by screaming at a certain pitch. Solid objects such as helmets or trees will block the attack. A chakra scream cannot be aimed and will only effect creatures in front of the user. 1pt. per Move + 1pt. per pt. of disruption. A Character must overcome the victim's hit points in the chosen area for the scream to work.

COMMAND VOICE: (20**BP**, 5**BP/**1pt.) Ability to command others with their voice. You can even command someone to kill him or herself. Half of **WILL** may save. Can only be directed at one victim at a time and requires that the victim understand the language used. 1pt per word.

ELECTRICAL RESISTANCE: (30**BP**, 5**BP/**1pt.) Causes Character to be resistant to electrical attack. 1pt. per pt. resisted + 1 pt. per Phase held.

ENHANCE MAGIC RESISTANCE: (30**BP**, 5**BP/**1pt.) Causes a temporary increase in the Character's magic resistance. 1pt. per pt. increase plus 2pts. per Phase held. Resists friendly and hostile magic.

HEALING TRANCE END/POWER/PSP/HIT: (50BP each. Specify) Gives an extra +1pt. per Round recovery each time taken. The trance lasts for 1 round. Multiple trances can be entered into simultaneously so long as they are not for the same effect (that is, you may go into *Healing Trance* for both **END** and **Hit** points, but not into two **END** trances).

HEIGHTENED HEARING: (20**BP**, 3**BP/**1pt.) Allows the Character to hear things normally too soft for people to hear (breathing, heartbeats etc.) 1pt. per 10'.

HEIGHTENED STR/CON/AG: (20**BP** each. Specify, 5**BP/**1pt.) Allows the Character to boost the specified attribute for one Phase. **END** costs are tripled. Effect is 1pt. of heightened **PA** per pt. boost. No **PA** can be boosted above 100. (Heightened **AG** is also called *celerity*.)

HEIGHTENED VISION: (20**BP**, 3**BP/**1pt) This ability enhances the visual abilities of the Character so that he or she can see everything in sharp focus and concentrate on all details, much like a hawk in search of prey. 1pt. per 10'.

INFRA VISION: (20**BP**, 3**BP/**1pt.) Allows Character to see areas of heat and cold, even in total darkness. This skill can be used with *Heightened Vision*, but not other visions. 1pt. per 10'.

NIGHT VISION: (20**BP**, 3**BP/**1pt.) Allows the Character to see at night or in low-light areas as though they are seeing on a cloudy day. This ability can be used with *Heightened Vision*, but not with other visions. 1pt. per 10'.

PAIN SONG: (20**BP**, 5**BP/**1pt.) Allows the Character to produce pain in all creatures within hearing range. Reduces skill use and **CNC** rolls by 50%. 1pt. per Move.

PSI RESISTANCE: (30**BP**, 5**BP/**1pt.) Similar to *Enhance Magic Resistance*, except this skill is used against psions.

RESIST COLD: (20**BP**, 3**BP/**1pt.) Gives the Character the ability to resist damage from extremely cold temperatures for short periods of time (2pts. per Round) or stops cold damage(1pt. of *Resist Cold* per pt. deflected).

RESIST HEAT: (20**BP**, 3**BP/**1pt.) Gives the Character the ability to resist damage from extremely hot temperatures for short periods of time (2pt. per Round) or stops heat damage (1pt. of *Resist Heat* per pt. deflected).

SONIC BLAST: (20**BP**, 5**BP**/1pt.) Does physical damage to objects or creatures. Victim must be in front of user. 1pt. per pt. damage + 1pt. per 5'.

SPIRIT HEARING: (20**BP**, 3**BP**/1pt.) Allows the Character to hear what is happening on the spirit plane or to hear spirit beings. 1pt. per 10'.

SPIRIT VISION: (20**BP**, 3**BP**/1pt.) Lets the Character see onto the spirit plane. This skill cannot be used with other visions. 1pt. per 10'.

SPIRIT VOICE: (20**BP**, 3**BP**/1pt.) Lets the user speak to the spirit plane without being heard on the Prime Material Plane. 1pt. per word.

SUPERLEAP: (30**BP**, 3**BP**/1pt.) Allows a Character to leap 1 foot per pt. forward plus 1 foot per pt. upward.

TRUE HEARING: (20**BP**, 3**BP**/1pt.) Allows a Character to ignore illusionary sounds or to hear cloaked, silenced, or muffled sounds as they truly are so long as the distortion is magical in nature. 1pt. per 10'.

TRUE VISION: (20**BP**, 3**BP**/1pt.) Allows a Character to see through illusions so long as they are magical in nature. 1pt. per 10'.

WALLWALK: (20**BP**, 5**BP**/1pt.) Allows a Character to walk on ceilings or walls in defiance of gravity. Also allows for walking on ships' hulls in the vacuum of space. 1pt. per 10'.

WATERWALK: (20**BP**, 5**BP**/1pt.) Allows a Character to walk on water. 1 pt. per 10".

WIND PUSH: (20**BP**, 5**BP**/1pt.) Allows a Character to move objects with a blast of air 1pt. per unit or to boost small object speeds 1pt. per pound of push. Can be used to blow out flames, cause distractions, etc. Requires a physical motion such as a punch or kick.

EQUIPMENT LISTS

MONEY
OLD WORLD/FANTASY/FUTURE

One (**LP,SH,BR,CP,ER**) weighs .1 unit each. One (**GP,DGP**) weighs .5 unit each. One (**EP,SP,STP**) weighs .3 unit each. One (**PP,MP**) weighs .2 unit each.

10 lead (**LP**) = 1 bronze (**BR**)
10 copper (**CP**) = 1 Silver (**SP**)
10 gold (**GP**) = 1 electrum (**ELP**)
10 platinum (**PP**)= 1 mythril (**MP**)
1 elvish rin (**ER**) = 2 (**GP**)
10 shells (**SH**) = 1 (**LP**)

10 bronze (**BR**) = 1 copper (**CP**)
10 silver (**SP**) = 1 gold (**GP**)
10 electrum (**ELP**) = 1 platinum (**PP**)
1 dwarven gold (**DGP**) = 1 (**ELP**)
1 steel (**STP**) = 1 (**SP**)

Note: cr = credits, which is the money system used in high-tech game settings. The "**$**" price x 3 = credit price in most game worlds.)

GEMS

Since some Characters have trouble carrying large amounts of metal around, it is sometimes useful to carry gems instead. Gem size is used to determine weight and value (very small .05 unit, small .1 unit, medium .2 unit, large .3 unit, very large .4 unit. Chunks may vary in weight.)

Ornamental Stones

	1CP-1SP	**1SP-1GP**	**1GP-10GP**	**10GP-20GP**	**20GP+**
*Azurite	small	medium	large	very large	chunk
^Agate	small	medium	large	very large	chunk
*Lapis Lazuli	small	medium	large	very large	chunk
*Obsidian	small	medium	large	very large	chunk
+Quartz	medium	large	very large	chunk	large chunk
^Tiger eye	small	medium	large	very large	chunk

Semiprecious Stones

	1SP-1GP	**1GP-10GP**	**10GP-20GP**	**20GP-50GP**	**50GP+**
*Abalone	small	medium	large	very large	chunk
*Bloodstone	small	medium	large	very large	chunk
*Carnelian	small	medium	large	very large	chunk
*Chalcedony	small	medium	large	very large	chunk
^Chrysoprase	small	medium	large	very large	chunk
+Citrine	small	medium	large	very large	chunk
*Jasper	small	medium	large	very large	chunk
^Moonstone	medium	large	very large	chunk	large chunk
*Onyx	medium	large	very large	chunk	large chunk
+Rock Crystal	medium	large	very large	chunk	large chunk
^Star Quartz	medium	large	very large	chunk	large chunk
+Zircon	small	medium	large	vry.lg	chunk

** opaque ^ translucent +crystalline/transparent*

Fancy Stones

	10-20**GP**	20-50**GP**	50-100**GP**	100-150**GP**	150+**GP**
^Amber	small	medium	large	very large	chunk
+Alexandrite	small	medium	large	very large	chunk
+Amethyst	small	medium	large	very large	chunk
+Aquamarine	small	medium	large	very large	chunk
+Chrysoberyl	small	medium	large	very large	chunk
*Coral	small	medium	large	very large	chunk
+Garnet	small	medium	large	very large	chunk
^Jade	small	medium	large	very large	chunk
*Jet	small	medium	large	very large	chunk
*Pearl	very small	small	medium	large	very large

Precious Stones

	10-50**GP**	50-100**GP**	100-500**GP**	500-1000**GP**	1000**GP**+
+Diamond	very.small	small	medium	large	very large
+Emerald	very.small	small	medium	large	very large
+Jacinth	very.small	small	medium	large	very large
*Opal	very.small	small	medium	large	very large
+Ruby	very.small	small	medium	large	very large
+Sapphire	very small	small	medium	large	very large

** opaque ^ translucent +crystalline/transparent*

Ornamental Stones have 1 mana point per .1 unit. Semi-Precious Stones have 2 mana points per .1 unit. Fancy Stones have 3 mana points per .1 unit. Precious Stones have 4 mana points per.1 unit. Carving, superior cutting, cracks or flaws can increase or decrease mana in stones.

Each game supplement will include money systems which work for their settings if they are different from those listed above. If you create your own world, there will probably be minerals of value found only in certain regions which are exclusive to your game, or the value of money in one area might be completely different from within another. For example, in an area rich with gold but poor in iron, iron pieces may be of far greater worth than gold. On a planet which has little water, water would be extremely valuable.

As you can see, value is a very relative term, and the lists above are only meant as a guideline.

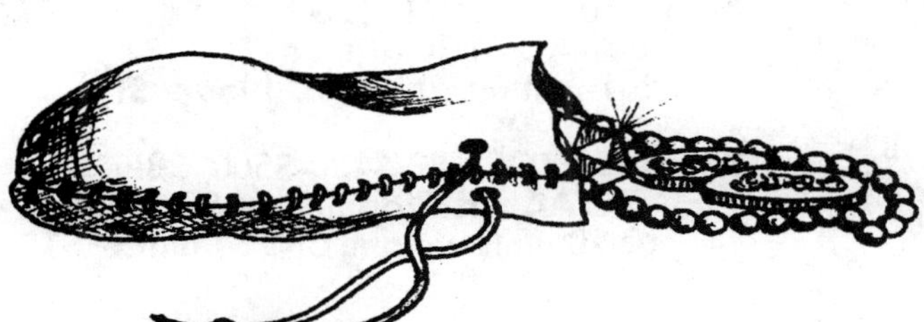

WEAPON DAMAGE

Weapon damage will change against various sizes of creatures.

Xtra Small	(XS)		[x5 damage]	-80% to hit
Very Small	(VS)	6"-2	[x4 damage]	-50% to hit
Small	(S)	2'-5	[x2 damage]	-30% to hit
Normal	(N)	5'-8	[normal]	- 0% to hit
Large	(L)	8'-20'	[1/2 damage]	+20% to hit
Very Large	(VL)	20+	[1/4 damage]	+40% to hit
Xtra Large	(XL)		[1/10 damage]	+60% to hit

Note: All Characters consider their own size to be normal. So for *Large* Characters, *Normal*-size Characters are considered *Small,* and the *Large* Character's weapon will do double damage to the *Normal*-size Character. The *Normal*-size Character can only do half damage to the *Large* Character in return. Can you say "It's a good time to run away?"

WEAPONS CHARTS

Basic Weapons

All weapons in any class are purchased seperately and have their own buy ratio. You may use *Buy Points* to purchase the weapon during Character generation, and this price is listed by the weapon in its description. The *Buy Points* for each weapon are listed as is its cost in cash. All weapons are at 98% to penetrate **AC** 0, there is a **AC** penalty listed. A Character should choose a weapon which weighs his/her **STR** or less for two-handed, or *half* their **STR** or less for one-handed handling. If you choose to ignore this statistic when purchasing weapons for your Character, be prepared to suffer a -1 **AG** penalty for each extra 5 units weight.

BLADES:

(**ONE-HANDED BLADES**) 30**BP**, 3pt./1pt.

Cutlass: (5**GP**-1**EP**/$75-$125, 10**BP**)
-5%/**AC**, 1**d12**+8 damage, -30%/3' thrown, 6-12 units weight, 2'-3' blade, **STR**, slash

Dagger: (5**CP**-10**GP**/ $5-$30, 5**BP**)
-10%/**AC**, 1**d8** damage, -10%/3' thrown, .2-.5 units weight, 3"-6" blade, **AG**

Dagger, Long: (1**SP**-15**GP**/ $10-$50, 8**BP**)
-8%/**AC**, 1**d10** damage, -15%/3' thrown, .5-1 unit weight, 6"-1' blade, **AG**

Dagger, Parrying: (1**GP**-25**GP**/ $35-$100, 8**BP**)
-20%/**AC**, 1**d8** damage, -50%/3' thrown, .4-.8 unit weight, 6"-1' blade, **AG**, break weapon

Dagger, Throwing: (10**CP**- 20**SP**/ $10-$30, 10**BP**)
-20%/**AC**, 1**d8** damage, -10%/10' thrown, .5-1 unit weight, 4"-8" blade, **AG**

Falchion: (10**GP**-12**EP**/$200-$500, 10**BP**)
-5%/**AC**, 3**d8** damage, -50%/2' thrown, 10-22 units weight, 3'-4'blade, **STR**

Foil: (2**SP**-5**GP**/$125-$300, 5**BP**)
-20%/**AC**, 1**d8** damage, -50%/3' thrown, .5-3 units weight, 3'-5' blade, **AG**, thrusting

Hand Claw: (1**GP**-25**GP**/ $25-$50 each, 5**BP** each)
-10%/**AC**, 1**d8** damage, NA, .2-.5 units weight each, 4"-8" blades, **AG**

Katana: (10**GP**-14**EP**/$200-$500, 10**BP**)
-5%/**AC**, 1**d20**+5 damage, -50%/2' thrown, 5-12 units weight, 3'-4' blade, **AG**

Katar (punch): (1**GP**-25**GP**/ $20-$100, 10**BP**)
-5%/**AC**, 1**d10** damage, NA, .5-1 unit weight, 6"-8" blade, **STR**

Khopesh: (2**GP**-1**EP**/$120-$500, 5**BP**)
-5%/**AC**, 2**d12** damage, -50%/2' thrown, 10-20 units weight, 3'-3'6" blade, **STR**, slash

Ninja-to: (5**GP**-7**EP**/$150-$300, 10**BP**)
-5%/**AC**, 1**d20**+4 damage, -50%/3' thrown, 5-10 units weight, 3'-4' blade, **AG**

***Plasma Blade**: (NA/$200-$1000, 20**BP**)
-1%/**AC**, 1**d12** damage, -50%/2' thrown, .2-.5 unit weight, 6"-8" blade, **AG**

***Plasma Sword**: (NA/$1000-$3000, 20**BP**)
-1%/**AC**, 1**d20**+10 damage, -60%/1' thrown, .5-1 unit weight, 3'-4' blade, **AG**

***Power Blade**: (NA/$300-$1000, 20**BP**)
-1%/**AC**, 2**d8** damage, -50%/2' thrown, .2-.5 unit weight, 6"-8" blade, **AG**

***Power Sword**: (NA/$3000-$5000, 30**BP**)
-1%/**AC**, 4**d10** damage, Throwing NA, .5-1 unit weight, 4'-5' blade, **AG**

Rapier: (12**GP**-20**EP**/$150-$500, 10**BP**)
-10%/**AC**, 1**d20** damage, -50%/1' thrown, 2-5 units weight, 3'6"-5' blade, **AG**, thrusting

Saber/Scimitar: (10**GP**-14**EP**/ $75-$350, 10**BP**)
-5%/**AC**, 1**d20** damage, -50%/2' thrown, 5-12 units weight, 3'-4'6" blade, **AG**

Sai: (1**SP**-10**SP**/$20-$75, 5**BP**)
-10%/**AC**, 1**d8** damage, -20%/3' thrown, .5-1 unit weight, 6"-10" blade, **AG** thrusting

Scythe: (1**SP**-1**GP**/$50-$125, 10**BP**)
-2%/**AC**, 2**d12** damage, -50%/1' thrown, 8-16 units weight, 3'-4'blade, **STR**, slash

Sickle: (5**CP**-10**SP**/$40-$80, 5**BP**)
-5%/**AC**, 1**d8** damage, -30%/2' thrown, .4-1 unit weight, 6"-10" blade, **AG**, slash

Stiletto: (1**SP**-12**GP**/$20-$75, 5**BP**)
-15%/**AC**, 1**d6** damage, -10%/3' thrown, .2-.6 unit weight, 3"-6" blade, **AG**, spring load, thrusting

Switch Blade: (10**GP**-40**GP**/$10-$50, 8**BP**)
-10%/**AC**, 1**d8** damage, -20%/3' thrown, .3-.8 unit weight, 3"-6" blade, **AG**, spring load

Sword, Broad: (10**GP**-14**EP**/$100-$300, 10**BP**)
-5%/**AC**, 1**d20**+4 damage, -50%/3' thrown, 5-12 units weight, 3'-4' blade, **AG**

Sword, Long: (14**GP**-20**EP**/$200-$500, 15**BP**)
-2%/**AC**, 2**d10**+2 damage, -50%/3' thrown, 10-20 units weight, 4'-5'blade, **AG** or **STR**

Sword, Short: (5**GP**-1**EP**/ $30-$150, 10**BP**)
-5%/**AC**, 1**d12**+5 damage, -20%/3' thrown, 1.5-3 units weight, 1'6"-3' blade, **AG**

(TWO-HANDED BLADE) 30**BP**, 5pt./1pt.

No-daichi: (30**GP**-8**PP**/$500-$3000, 20**BP**)
-1%/**AC**, 1**d10**+20 damage, -100%/2' thrown, 15-30 units weight, 5'6"-6' blade, **STR**

Scythe, Great: (5**GP**-1**EP**/$300-$800, 20**BP**)
-1%/**AC**, 3**d10**+5 damage, Throwing NA, 15-30 units weight,, 6'-7' handle/3'-3'6"blade, **STR**, slash

Sword, Great: (50**GP**-10**PP**/$800-$2000, 20**BP**)
-2%/**AC**, 1**d10**+20 damage, -100%/3' thrown, 20-40 units weight, 5'6"-6' blade, **STR**

Sword, Knight's: (20**GP**- 25**EP**/$300-$1000, 15**BP**)-2%/**AC**, 2**d10**+8 damage, -80%/3' thrown, 14-30 units weight, 5'-5'6" blade, **STR**

CHAIN/ROPE 30**BP**, 3pt./1pt.

Bolas: (10**CP**-8**SP**/$30-$125, 10**BP**)
-20%/**AC**, 2**d6** damage, -10%/5'thrown, .5-2 units weight, 3'radius, **AG**, blunt/tangl

Bullwhip: (1**SP**-3**GP**/$10-$35, 5**BP**)
-20%/**AC**, 1**d8** damage, Throwing NA, .5-1 unit weight, 4'-10', **AG**

Cat of 9 Tails: (5**SP**-10**GP**/$75-$200, 8**BP**)
-20%/**AC**, 1**d8** damage, Throwing NA, 1-5 units weight, 4'-6', **AG**, tangle

Chain: (5**CP**-5**SP**/$5-$15, 5**BP**)
-20%/**AC**, 1**d8** damage, Throwing NA, 1-3 units weight, 3'-4', **AG**, blunt

Chain Whip: (3**GP**-10**GP**/$25-$50, 10**BP**)
-10%/**AC**, 1**d10** damage, Throwing NA, 2-4 units weight, 3'-4', **AG**, blunt

Flail: (5**SP**-12**GP**/$75-$350, 20**BP**)
-5%/**AC**, 2**d12** damage, Throwing NA, 5-12 units weight, 3'6"- 5', **AG** or **STR**, blunt/spike

Garrote: (1**CP**-1**GP**/$0-$5, 5**BP**)
-20%/**AC**, 1**d6** damage, Throwing NA, .2 unit weight, 3', **STR**, strangle

Kusarigama: (15**GP**-50**GP**/$75-$200, 20**BP**)
-10%/**AC**, 2**d12** damage, Throwing NA, 8-12 units weight, 6'-8', **AG**, blunt/cut/hook

Kyogetsu Shoge: (8**GP**-30**GP**/ $50-$150, 15**BP**)
-10%/**AC**, 1**d10**+5 damage, Throwing NA, 5-8 units weight, 6', **AG**, blunt/hook

Lasso: (1**CP**-1**SP**/$5-$20, 5**BP**)
-30%/**AC**, 1**d6** damage, Throwing NA, .5-1unit weight, 6'-12', **AG**, strangle/bind

Manriki Gusari: (1**SP**-5**GP**/$25-$75, 10**BP**)
-10%/**AC**, 1**d10** damage, Throwing NA 1-3 units weight, 3', **AG**, blunt/ strangle

***Neuro Bolas**: (NA/$800-$2000, 30**BP**)
-20%/**AC**, 2**d10**+4 damage, -10%/5' thrown, .5 unit weight, 3' radius, **AG**, nerve attack

***Neuro Whip**: (NA/$1000-$3000, 30**BP**)
-20%/**AC**, 3**d10** damage, Throwing NA, .5-1 unit weight, 4'-10', **AG**, nerve attack

Nunchakus: (1**EP**-1**PP**/$10-$50, 10**BP**)
-20%/**AC**, 3**d6** damage, -50%/3' thrown, 1 unit weight, 1' (3'extended), **AG**, blunt

Scourge: (5**GP**-25**GP**/$45-$200, 20**BP**)
-10%/**AC**, 1**d20**+5 damage, -50%/3' thrown 1-3 units weight, 4'-10', **AG**, spikes

3 Section Staff: (1**SP**-8**GP**/ $50-$125, 10**BP**)
-20%/**AC**, 3**d6** damage, Throwing NA, 5-8 units weight, 1'6"(6'extended), **AG**, blunt

CLUBS/AXES/MACES

(**ONE-HANDED CLUBS/ETC.**) 30**BP**,3pt./1pt.

Axe, Hand: (10**SP**-5**GP**/$5-$15, 5**BP**)
-10%/**AC**, 1**d20** damage, -10%/3' thrown, 2-6 units weight, 1'-3' length, **STR**

Billy Club/Tonfa: (1**SP**-5**GP**/$15-$35, 10**BP**)
-20%/**AC**, 1**d10** damage, -10%/5' thrown, 1-2 units weight, 12"-18" length, **STR**, blunt

Club: (0**CP**-10**CP**/$0-$5, 2**BP**)
-20%/**AC**, 1**d10** damage, -20%/3' thrown, 1-3 units weight, 3' stick, **STR**, blunt

***Club, Neuro**: (NA/$125-$300, 25**BP**)
-20%/**AC**, 2**d12** damage, -10%/3' thrown, 1-1.5 units weight, 12"-18" length, **AG**, stun-pain

Hammer, Knight's: (5**GP**-20**EP**/$100-$500, 20**BP**)
-2%/**AC**, 2**d12** damage, Throwing NA 10-15 units weight, 3'-5' length, **STR**

Hammer, War: (2**GP**-16**GP**/$100-$500, 20**BP**)
-5%/**AC**, 2**d8** damage, -15%/3' thrown, 5-10 units weight, 1'6"-3' length, **STR**

Mace: (2**SP**-12**GP**/$15-$35, 5**BP**)
-10%/**AC**, 2**d8** damage, -15%/3' thrown, 4-10 units weight, 1'6"-3' length, **STR**

***Mace, Force**: (NA/ $300-$600, 30**BP**)
-10%/**AC**, 2**d12** damage, -15%/3' thrown, 2-3 units weight, 1'6"-3' length, **AG**, blunt

Mace, Horseman's: (1**GP**-12**EP**/$50-$300, 20**BP**)
-5%/**AC**, 2**d12** damage, Throwing NA, 10-15 units weight, 3'-5' length, **STR**

Metal Pipe: (1**SP**-1**GP**/$0-$20, 5**BP**)
-10%/**AC**, 2**d6** damage, -20%/3' thrown, 1.5-3 units weight, 1'-3' length, **STR**

Pick: (10**SP**-30**GP**/$50-$100, 20**BP**)
-5%/**AC**, 2**d12** damage, -40%/5' thrown, 5-12 units weight, 3'-4' length, **STR**, puncture

Pick, Cavalry: (5**GP**-10**EP**$100-$500, 30**BP**)
-2%/**AC**, 3**d10** damage, Throwing NA, 12-20 units weight, 4'-5' length, **STR**, puncture

Sap: (5**CP**-1**SP**/$5-$10, 5**BP**)
-20%/**AC**, 1**d8** damage, Throwing NA, .5-1.5 units weight, 8"-1' length, **STR**

***Stun Stick**: (NA/ $75-$200, 20**BP**)
Special, 1**d20**+10 stun/electrical, -10%/3' thrown, 1-2 units weight, 12"-18" length, **AG**, electrical stun

(**TWO-HANDED CLUBS, ETC.**) 30**BP**, 5pt./1pt.

Axe, Battle: (14**EP**-12**PP**/$1000-$3000, 30**BP**)
-2%/**AC**, 3**d10**+4 damage, Throwing NA, 10-20 units weight, 4'-6' length, **STR**

Hammer, Battle: (15**GP**-50**EP**/$500-$1000, 30**BP**)
-2%/**AC**, 4**d10** damage, Throwing NA, 15-30 units weight, 3'6"-5'6" length, **STR**

Mace, Heavy: (1**GP**-18**GP**/$500-$2000, 30**BP**)
-2%/**AC**, 1**d12**+5 damage, Throwing NA, 10-20 units weight, 4'-5'6" length, **STR**, blunt

Morning Star: (1**GP**-15**GP**/ $400-$800, 25**BP**)
-2%/**AC**, 3**d10** damage, Throwing NA, 10-20 units weight, 3'6"-5' length, **STR**, puncture

Pick, War: (15**GP**-50**EP**/$800-$1500, 30**BP**)
-1%/**AC**, 4**d10** damage, Throwing NA, 20-30 units weight, 4'-6' length, **STR**, puncture

FIST LOADS: 20BP, 3pt./1pt.

Brass Knuckles: (5**CP**-2**SP**/ $3-$10, 5**BP**)
-5%/**AC**, 1**d6** damage + blow damage, Throwing NA, .5 unit weight, 4-6" length, **STR**

Cestus/Spiked Glove: (3**SP**-8**GP**/$10-$35, 10**BP**
-2%/**AC**, 1**d10**+blow damage, Throwing NA,
.5 unit weight, 4-6" length, **STR**

Fist Load/Small Rod: (0**CP**-5**CP**/ $0-$5, 2**BP**)
-20%/**AC**, 1**d6**+blow damage, Throwing NA,
.1 unit weight, 4-6" length, **STR**

Knuckle Knife: (1**SP**-4**GP**/$15-$50, 8**BP**)
-2%/**AC**, 1**d8**+blow damage, Throwing NA,
.5 unit weight, 4-6" length, **STR**

Sandbag: (2**CP**-1**SP**/$1-$5, 5**BP**)
-10%/**AC**, 1**d8** damage, Throwing NA,
.5 unit weight, 6-10" length, **STR**

Shuko: (5**SP**-10**GP**/$12-$40, 10**BP**)
-2%/**AC**, 1**d8**+blow damage, Throwing NA,
.5 unit weight, 4-6" length, **STR**

***Zapper**: (NA/$15-$40, 5**BP**)
Special, 1**d20**+10 stun/electrical, Throwing NA, .5 unit weight, 4-6"length, **AG**

POLE ARMS:

(ONE-HANDED POLE ARMS) 20**BP**, 3pt./1pt.

Javelin: (1**SP**-5**GP**/$45-$125, 15**BP**)
-5%/**AC**, 1**d12**+2 damage, -5%/15' thrown,
2-4 units weight, 4'-6' length, **STR**

Spear: (3**CP**-10**SP**/$25-$100,10**BP**)
-5%/**AC**, 1**d12** damage, -5%/10' thrown,
1.5-3.5 units weight, 4'-6' length, **STR**

Staff, Short: (0**CP**-5**SP**/$5-$45, 5**BP**)
-20%/**AC**, 1**d10** damage,-20%/5' thrown,
1-3 units weight, 3'6"-4'6" length, **STR**

Trident: (5**SP**-8**GP**/$30-$100, 12**BP**)
-5%/**AC**, 1**d12**+5 damage, -10%/10' thrown,
2-4 units weight, 4'-6' length, **STR**

(TWO-HANDED POLE ARMS) 30**BP**, 3pt./1pt.

Glaive: (2**GP**-10**EP**/$75-$300, 20**BP**)
-4%/**AC**, 3**d6**+2 damage, -12%/10' thrown,
10-14 units weight, 6-8' length, **STR**

Halberd: (10**GP**-20**EP**/$100-$400, 22**BP**)
-2%/**AC**, 2**d10**+4 damage, -20%/10' thrown,
12-16 units weight, 6-8' length, **STR**

Harpoon: (5**CP**-10**SP**/$25-$100, 10**BP**)
-5%/**AC**, 1**d12** damage, -5%/10' thrown,
2-4 units weight, 3-5' length, **STR**

Lance: (1**EP**-20**EP**/$200-$500, 20**BP**)
-2%/**AC**, 3**d10** damage, Throwing NA,
8-12 units weight, 6-8' length, **STR**

Mancatcher: (5**SP**-1**EP**/$50-$150, 10**BP**)
AC NA, 1**d4** damage, Throwing NA,
6-10 units weight, 4-6' length, **STR**, entangle

Pike/Long Spear: (5**SP**-15**GP**/$50-$250, 15**BP**)
-5%/**AC**, 2**d8**+2 damage, -10%/10' thrown,
8-12 units weight, 6-8' length, **STR**

Staff, Long: (1**SP**-5**GP**/$30-$200, 12**BP**)
-15%/**AC**, 3**d6** damage, -25%/5' thrown,
4-8 units weight, 6-8' length, **STR**

Staff, Quarter: (5**CP**-1**GP**/$15-$100, 8**BP**)
-15%/**AC**, 1**d12** damage, -20%/5' thrown,
2-4 units weight, 4-6' length, **STR**

BOWS/SLINGS:

*(**STR** bonus/penalties do not apply to some of these weapons as noted in description.)* 30**BP**,5pt./1pt.

Bow, Hunting: (10**SP**-20**GP**/ $50-$125, 15**BP**)
-8%/**AC**, 3**d6** damage, -5%/15',
4-6 units weight, 3'-5' length, **STR**

Bow, Long: (14**GP**-20**EP**/$100-$500, 20**BP**)
-5%/**AC**, 2**d10** damage, -2%/20',
5-8 units weight, 5'-7' length, **STR**

Bow, Short: (6**SP**-12**GP**/$25-$75, 10**BP**)
-10%/**AC**, 2**d8** damage, -5%/10',
2-4 units weight, 2'-3' length, **STR**

Crossbow/Harpoon Gun: (14**EP**-20**PP**/$100-$500,30**BP**) -5%/**AC**, 2**d12** damage,
-5%/15',6-10 units weight, 3'-4' length, **AG**,
STR bonus NA

Crossbow, Double: (20**EP**-25**PP**/$200-$800,
35**BP**) -5%/**AC**, 2**d12** damage, -5%/15',
8-12 units weight, 3'-4' length, **AG**, **STR** bonus NA

Crossbow, Heavy: (20**EP**-25**PP**/$200-$800, 35**BP**)
-2%/**AC**, 2**d12**+4 damage, -2%/15',
12-16 units weight, 4'-4'6" length, **AG**, **STR** bonus NA

Crossbow, Mini: (5**PP**-20**MP**/$75-$300, 30**BP**)
-10%/**AC**, 2**d8** damage, -10%/15',
1-3 units weight, 1'-2' length, **AG**, **STR** bonus NA

***Crossbow, Neuro**: (NA/800cr-2000cr, 35**BP**)
Special, 2**d20** electrical/stun, -5%/10',
3-4 units weight, **AG**, **STR** bonus NA, 6 charges per clip

***Crossbow, Photon**: (NA/1000cr-3000cr, 80**BP**)
-2%/5**AC**, 3**d20** damage, -5%/20',
3-6 units weight, **AG**, **STR** bonus NA, 2
charges per clip

***Crossbow, Plasma**: (NA/900cr-2800cr, 70**BP**)
-5%/2**AC**, 3**d20** damage, -5%/20',
3-6 units weight, **AG**, **STR** bonus NA, 3
charges per clip

Crossbow, Repeating: (50**EP**-50**PP**/$200-$800,
40**BP**) -10%/**AC**, 2**d8** damage, -10%/15',
8-12 units weight, 3'-4' length, **AG**, **STR** bonus
NA, 6 quarrel clips

***Crossbow, Taser**: (NA/300cr-600cr, 30**BP**)
Special, 1**d20**+5 electrical/stun, -5%/10',
3-4 units weight, **AG**, **STR** bonus NA, 12
charges per clip

Sling: (0**CP**-1**SP**/$5-$25, 5**BP**)
-10%/**AC**, 1**d6** damage, -5%/10,
.5 unit weight, 1-3' length, **STR** or **AG**

ˆSling Shot: (NA/$1-$20, 5**BP**)
-10%/**AC**, 1**d8** damage, -5%/15',
.5 unit weight, 8-10" length, **STR**

GUNS:*(**STR** bonus/penalty NA to damage)*
(ONE-HANDED GUNS) 30**BP**, 5pt./1pt.

***Air Blaster**: (NA/100cr-200cr, 10**BP**)
Special, 1**d10**move stun, -1%/2',
.5 unit weight, 6"-8", **AG**, unlimited ammo

Astra 9mm: (NA/$50-$100, 25**BP**)
-5%/2**AC**, 3**d6** damage, -2%/15',
.5 unit weight, 6"-7", **AG**, 15-shot magazine

Ball Pistol: (NA/$25-$175, 25**BP**)
-5%/2**AC**, 3**d6** damage, -2%/10',
3 units weight, 8-12", **AG**, 1-shot load

Beretta 9mm: (NA/$40-$100, 30**BP**)
-5%/2**AC**, 3**d6** damage, -2%/15',
2 units weight, 6", **AG**, 13-shot magazine

***Blaster (Particle Beam)**: (NA/ 2000cr-6000cr,
80**BP**) -1%/5**AC**, 2**d10**+5 damage, -5%/10',
.8 unit weight, 6"-8", **AG**,
6 blasts per charge pack

Calico 9mm: (NA/$125-$350, 50**BP**)
-5%/2**AC**, 3**d6** damage, -2%/15',
3 units weight, 12 -15", **AG**, 50-shot magazine

Colt .38 Special: (NA/$50-$200, 30**BP**)
-1%/**AC**, 2**d8** damage, -2%/15',
2 units weight, 6"-7", **AG**, 6-shot revolver

***Disrupter**: (NA/4000cr-8000cr, 50**BP**)
-1%/5**AC**, 3**d10** damage, -10%/25',
2 units weight, 8"-10", **AG**,
4 blasts per charge pack

***Flamer Gun**: (NA/800cr-2000cr, 40**BP**)
-2%/**AC**, 2**d8** fire damage, -10%/20',
2 units weight, 10"-12", **AG**, 10 blasts per tank

***Laser Gun**: (NA/1500cr-3000cr, 40**BP**)
-1%/2**AC**, 1**d20** damage, -1%/50',
1 unit weight, 6"-8", **AG**,
4 blasts per charge pack

Magnum .357: (NA/ $35-$75, 30**BP**)
-2%/2**AC**, 2**d10** damage, -2%/15',
3 units weight, 8", **AG**, 6-shot revolver

***Needle Gun**: (NA/200cr-800cr, 25**BP**)
-1%/**AC**, 1**d10**/burst damage, -5%/15',
.3 unit weight, 4"-6", **AG**, 4 bursts per clip

***Phaser**: (NA/5000cr-10000cr, 50**BP**)
-1%/10**AC**, 5**d6**+5 stun/kill damage, -5%/25',
.5 unit weight, 8"-10", **AG**,
12 blasts per charge pack

***Photon Pistol**: (NA/5000cr-10000cr, 100**BP**)
-1%/5**AC**, 3**d10** damage, -1%/50',
1.5 units weight, 10"-12", **AG**,
6 blasts per charge pack

Pistol, .22 cal.: (NA/$35-$125, 15**BP**)
-10%/2**AC**, 2**d6** damage, -5%/15',
.5-1 unit weight, 3"-5", **AG**, 7-shot clip

***Plasma Gun**: (NA/6000cr-12000cr, 70**BP**)
-1%/5**AC**, 3**d12** fire damage, -5%/15',
1 unit weight, 10"-12", **AG**, 10 blasts per tank

Revolver, .357: (NA/$35-$75, 30**BP**)
-2%/2**AC**, 2**d10** damage, -2%/15',
3 units weight, 8", **AG**, 6-shot revolver

Revolver, 9mm: (NA/$40-$100, 20**BP**)
-5%/2**AC**, 3**d6** damage, -2%/15',
1-2 units weight, 4"-6", **AG**, 7-shot revolver

Revolver, .45 cal.: (NA/$50-$200, 35**BP**)
-1%/2**AC**, 2**d10**+4 damage, -2%/15',
2-4 units weight, 8-10", **AG**, 6-shot revolver

***Rocket Pistol**: (NA/800cr-1500cr, 45**BP**)
-1%/2**AC**, 2**d10** explosive, -2%/30',
2.5 units weight, 12"-14", **AG**,
2 rockets per clip

Ruger, 9mm: (NA/$50-$125, 25**BP**)
-5%/2**AC**, 3**d6** damage, -2%/15',
.8 unit weight, 7"-8", **AG**,
15-shot magazine

***Sonic Gun**: (NA/600cr-1000cr, 20**BP**)
-5%/**AC**, 1**d8** sound damage, -10%/20',
.5 unit weight, 6"-8", **AG**,
5 blasts per charge pack

***Tangle Gun**: (NA/100cr-300cr, 20**BP**)
Special, no damage, -5%/10',
.8 unit weight, 8"-10", **AG**, 2 nets per clip

***Taser Gun**: (NA/100cr-300cr, 20**BP**)
-5%/**AC**, 1**d10** electrical/stun, -10%/5',
.5 unit weight, 6"-8", **AG**, 1 barb per clip

Walther PPK: (NA/ $35-$75, 20**BP**)
-10%/2**AC**, 2**d8** damage, -2%/10',
.5 unit weight, 4.5", **AG**, 7-shot magazine

(SUBMACHINE/MACHINE GUNS) 50BP,5pt./1pt.

Ares 9mm: (NA/$800-$1000, 35**BP**)
-5%/2**AC**, 3**d6** damage/bullet, -5%/20',
1.5 units weight, 6"x4"x2.5" folded/12"-14"
unfolded, 32-shot magazine, **AG**,
8-shot short bursts

Ceska Skorpion: (NA/$500-$1000, 40**BP**)
-5%/2**AC**, 2**d8**+2 damage/bullet, -5%/20',
1.4 units weight, 8"x5"x3"folded/
16"-18"unfolded, 20-shot magazine, **AG**,
10 shot short bursts, 100-shot belt feed

CNI: (NA/$800-$1500, 45**BP**)
-5%/2**AC**, 2**d10** damage/bullet, -5%/20',
3 units weight, 2'x6"x3" folded/3'6"-4'
unfolded, 30-shot magazine, **AG**,
10-shot short bursts, built-in silencer

Micro Uzi: (NA/$1000-$3000, 35**BP**)
-5%/2**AC**, 3**d6** damage/bullet, -5%/25',
1 unit weight, , 6.5"x4"x2.5" folded
/10"-14"unfolded, **AG**,
20-shot magazine, 5- shot short bursts

Mini Uzi: (NA/ $1500-$3500, 35**BP**)
-5%/2**AC**, 3**d6** damage/bullet, -5%/25',
1.8 units weight,, 8"x4"x2.5" folded/16"
unfolded, **AG**, 20-shot magazine,
5-shot short bursts, 100-shot belt feed

Uzi: (NA/$3000-$5000, 40**BP**)
-5%/2**AC**, 3**d6** damage/bullet, -5%/20',
2.2 units weight, 10"x4.5"x3"folded/
16"-20"unfolded, **AG**, 32-shot magazine,
8- shot short bursts, 200-shot belt feed

(TWO-HANDED GUNS) 50BP, 5pt./1pt.

Arquebus: (12**PP**-24**PP**/$300-$500, 35**BP**)
-5%/2**AC**, 3**d6** damage/ball, -5%/15',
6 units weight, 3'6" length, **AG**,
ball-and- powder load

Benelli 121 M1: (NA/$300-$600, 80**BP**)
-5%/3**AC**, 3**d12** damage/shot, -5%/20',
6 units weight, 3'6"-4' length, **AG**,
7-shot, semi-automatic pump

Beretta Sniper: (NA/$1000-$2000, 70**BP**)
-5%/2**AC**, 3**d10** damage/shot, -2%/125',
6 units weight, 4'6"-6' length, **AG**,
5-shot, bolt

***Blaster Rifle (Particle Beam)**:(NA/4000cr-10000cr,100**BP**) -1%/5**AC**, 3**d10**+5 damage,
-5%/30',3 units weight, 3'-4' length, **AG**,
10 blasts per charge pack

Browning .50 cal. Rifle: (NA/$1000-$2000, 75**BP**)
-5%/2**AC**, 3**d12** damage/shot, -5%/125',
6.5 units weight, 4'-6' length, **AG**,
5-shot, bolt

***Disrupter Rifle**: (NA/ 8000cr-12000cr, 100**BP**)
-1%/5**AC**, 4**d10** damage, -5%/25',
8 units weight, 3'6"-5' length, **AG**,
8 blasts per charge pack

Elephant Gun: (NA/$1500-$2500, 80**BP**)
-5%/4**AC**, 3**d10**+7 damage/shot, -5%/12',
8 units weight, 3'6"-4'6" length, **AG**,
5-shot, pump

***Flamer Defender**: (NA/3000cr-6000cr, 75**BP**)
-2%/**AC**, 2**d10** fire damage, -5%/25',
8 units weight, 3'-4' length, **AG**,
20 blasts per tank

Flintlock: (100**PP**-125**PP**/$600-$1500, 40**BP**)
-5%/2**AC**, 3**d8** damage/ball, -5%/30',
6 units weight, 4'-6'length, **AG**, ball-and-powder load

Grenade Gun: (NA/ $2500-$4000, 90**BP**)
-5%/4**AC**, 2**d10**+20 explosive, -5%/10'
8 units weight, 3'-4' length, **AG**, 3-shot, pump

***Laser Rifle**: (NA/1000cr-2500cr, 50**BP**)
-1%/3**AC**, 1**d20** damage, -2%/110',
2 units weight, 2'-3' length, **AG**,
8 blasts per charge pack

Musket: (24**PP**-48**PP**/$400-$800, 40**BP**)
-5%/2**AC**, 3**d8** damage/ball, -5%/20',
6 units weight, 3'6"-4'6" length, **AG**,
ball-and- powder load

***Needle Rifle**: (NA/800cr-1000cr, 35**BP**)
-1%/**AC**, 1**d12**/burst damage, -5%/20',
1 unit weight, 2'-3' length, **AG**,
6 bursts per clip

***Phaser Rifle**: (NA/10000cr-15000cr, 100**BP**)
-1%/10**AC**, **3d10**+10 stun/kill damage,
-5%/50', 3 units weight, 3' length, **AG**,
24 blasts per charge pack

***Photon Repeater**: (NA/2500cr-5000cr, 90**BP**)
-1%/5**AC**, **3d10**+5 damage, -1%/100'
6 units weight, 2'-3' length, **AG**,
12 blasts per charge pack.

***Plasma Repeater**: (NA/12000cr-18000cr, 95**BP**)
-1%/5**AC**, **4d12** fire damage, -5%/25',
5 units weight, 2'6"-3'6" length, **AG**,
20 blasts per tank

Rifle, Counterterrorist AI PM: (NA/$800-$1500,
65**BP**) -5%/2**AC**, **3d8** damage/shot, -5%/100',
7 units weight, 4'6" length, **AG**,
10-shot, bolt

***Rocket Rifle**: (NA/ 2000cr-5000cr, 100**BP**)
-5%/4**AC**, **2d10**+25 explosive, -5%/50',
5 units weight, 3'-4' length, **AG**,
4 rockets per clip

Shotgun, 12 gauge: (NA/$200-$500, 50**BP**)
-5%/3**AC**, **3d12** damage/shot, -5%/20',
6 units weight, 3'6"-4'6" length, **AG**,
1 shot load

Note: (2 shot, **double barrel** available: NA/$400-$800, 75**BP**), **pump** (sawed off: NA/$800-$1500, 75**BP**, +5 damage per shot, -20%/25', 3'-3'6" length,) **double-barrel pump** (same as above except 90**BP**)

***Sonic Rifle**: (NA/800cr-2000cr, 25**BP**)
-5%/**AC**, 1**d10** sound damage, -5%/20',
1.5 units weight, 1'-2'length, **AG**,
10 blasts per pack

***Tangle Rifle**: (NA/500cr-800cr, 25**BP**)
Special, no damage, -5%/20',
2.5 units weight, 3'-4' length, **AG**,
6 nets per clip

***Taser Rifle**: (NA/300cr-600cr, 25**BP**)
-5%/**AC**, 1**d10** electrical/stun, -10%/15',
2 units weight, 2'-3' length, **AG**,
3 barbs per clip

Winchester Defender 1300: (NA/$500-$1000, 85**BP**)
-5%/4**AC**, **3d12** damage/shot, -5%/15',
6 units weight, 3'6" length, **AG**,
7-shot, pump

SPECIALTY:

(ONE-HANDED SPECIALTY) 30**BP**, 3pt./1pt.

Blowgun: (5**CP**-1**SP**/$0-$100, 2**BP**)
1**d6**+blow damage (as fistload), NA,
.4 unit weight, 6"-3', **PA** NA

Boomerang: (0**CP**-2**SP**/ $0-$100, 20**BP**)
-20%/**AC**, 1**d8** damage, -5%/20',
1 unit weight, 1'-2', **STR**

Bottle: (0**CP**-1**GP**/$0-$5, 1**BP**)
-20%/**AC**, 1**d6** damage, -20%/5',
.5 unit weight, 8"-12", **STR**

Brick/Rock: (1**CP**-6**CP**/$0-$5, 1**BP**)
-10%/**AC**, 1**d8** damage, -10%/5',
1 unit weight, 8", **STR**

Caltrop: (2**CP**-10**CP**/$1-$5, 1**BP**)
-8%/**AC**, 1**d4** damage, NA,
.1 unit weight, 1", **PA** NA

Chemical Spray (Blinding): (NA/$5-$20, 10**BP**)
-20%/**AC**, No damage (blind 1**d20** Moves),
-25% /5', .2 unit weight, 3"-4" dispenser, **AG**,
2 shots

Chemical Spray (Corrosive): (NA/$50-$125, 20**BP**)
-20%/**AC**, 1**d8** damage, -25%/5',
.2 unit weight, 3"-4" dispenser, **AG**, 2 shots

Darts: (0**CP**-1**SP**/$5-$25, 2**BP**)
-10%/**AC**, 1**d6** damage, -5%/10',
.2 unit weight, 4"-6", **AG**

Exploding Eggs: (2**CP**-1**SP**/$5-$25, 2**BP**)
NA, No damage (blind/sneeze 1**d12** Moves),
-5%/10', .2 unit weight, 3" egg, **AG**

Fighting Cape: (24**SP**-10**GP**/$300-$1000, 10**BP**)
-5%/**AC**, 1**d10** damage or tangle, NA,
10 units weight, size varies, **AG**

Fighting Fan: (3**SP**-10**GP**/$75-$200, 5**BP**)
-10%/**AC**, 1**d8** damage, -20%/10',
1 unit weight, 8"-12", **AG**

Gaff Hook/Hook Hand: (5**CP**-5**SP**/$.50-$25, 5**BP**)
-10%/**AC**, 1**d8** damage, NA,
1.5 units weight, 6"-8", size varies, **STR**

Hand Grenade: (NA/$50-$300, 30**BP**)
-5%/4**AC**, 2**d10**+20 damage explosive,
-20%/10', .2 unit weight, 4" egg, **AG**

Letter Opener: (1**SP**-1**GP**/$5-$20, 2**BP**)
-10%/**AC**, 1**d6** damage, NA,
.3 unit weight, 5"- 8", **STR**

Long Pin/Hat Pin: (5**CP**-2**SP**/$5-$15, 4**BP**)
-10%/**AC**, 1**d6** damage, NA,
.2 unit weight, 6"-8", **AG**

Marbles: (1**CP**-5**CP**/ $.10-$.50, 1**BP**)
NA, no damage (Trip), NA,
.1-.2 units weight, .5"-1" sphere, **PA** NA

Net: (5**CP**-8**SP**/$15-$75, 2**BP**)
NA, No damage (Tangle), -1%/1',
3 units weight, 4' radius, **AG**

Pencil/Pen: (NA/$.25-$3, 1**BP**)
-15%/**AC**, 1**d6** damage, NA,
.1 unit weight, 3"-8", **STR**

Pool Ball: (5**CP**-1**SP**/$1-$5, 1**BP**)
-20%/**AC**, 1**d6** damage blunt, -1%/1',
1 unit weight, 3" sphere, **STR**

Pool Cue: (1**SP**-5**GP**/$20-$100, 2**BP**)
-20%/**AC**, 1**d8** damage, -20%/5',
1-3 units weight, 4'-5', **STR**

Rolling Pin: (5**CP**-1**SP**/ $0-$15, 2**BP**)
-20%/**AC**, 1**d8** damage, -20%/3',
2 units weight, 1'6"-2', **STR**

Shield: (10**GP**-20**PP**/$100-$500, 20**BP**)
-15%/**AC**, 1**d4** damage per 5 units weight of shield, weight varies, size varies, **STR**

Skillet: (1**SP**-1**GP**/$10-$25, 2**BP**)
-20%/**AC**, 1**d10** damage, -20%/5',
4 units weight, 10"radius, **STR**

Sling Staff: see **Sling** and **Short Staff**

Spike/Piton: (5**CP**-1**SP**/ $3-$5, 3**BP**)
-5%/**AC**, 1**d10** damage, NA,
1 unit weight, 8"-12", **STR**

Throwing Stars: (5**SP**-1**GP**/$5-$15, 5**BP**)
-10%/**AC**, 1**d8** damage, -10%/20',
.2 unit weight, 3.5" radius, **AG**

Wind/Fire Wheel: (1**SP**-10**GP**/$50-$125,10**BP**)
-5%/**AC**, 1**d8** damage, NA,
1 unit weight, 12" arc, **AG**, slash

Yo-Yo: (3**CP**-8**CP**/$1-$5, 4**BP**)
-10%/**AC**, 1**d6** damage, string length range,
.3 unit weight, 3"radius, **AG**

(**Note**: *Explosive damage from any explosive weapon is reduced by 1pt/ft. from ground zero.*)

ARMOR

Arm Guards, Forearm, Metal:
1**EP**-5**EP**($75-200) 3 units weight/each

Arm Guards, Forearm, Plastic:
NA($10-35) .5 unit weight/each

Arm Guards, Upper Arm, Metal:
1**EP**-5**EP**($75-200) 3 units weight/each

Arm Guards, Upper Arm, Plastic:
NA($10-35) .5 unit weight/each

Back Plate, Metal:
5**EP**-1**PP**($800-2K) 30 units weight

Back Plate, Plastic:
NA($75-300) 5 units weight

Barding, Chainmail (Mount):
1**PP**-5**PP** 60 units weight

Barding, Hardened Leather (Mount):
5**EP**-1**PP** 15 units weight

Barding, Plate (Mount):
5**PP**-15**PP** 150 units weight

Boots, Ankle-High, Hardened Leather:
5**SP**-1**GP**($35-75) 3 units weight/pair

Boots, Knee-High, Hardened Leather:
1**GP**-5**GP**($50-250) 4 units weight/pair

Boots, Thigh-High, Hardened Leather:
5**GP**-1**EP**($125-500) 8 units weight/pair

Boots, Plate, Metal:
5**EP**-1**PP**($350-1K) 5 units weight/each

Boots, Plate, Plastic:
NA($35-100) 1 unit weight/each

Breast Plate, Metal:
5**EP**-1**PP**($800-2K) 30 units weight

Breast Plate, Plastic:
NA($75-300) 5 units weight

Coat, Trench, Kevlar:
NA($1K-5K) 6 units weight

Gauntlets, Leather:
5**SP**-1**GP**($100-300) 1 unit weight/pair

Gauntlets, Leather w/ Plate:
2**GP**-5**GP**($250-500) 4 units weight/pair

Helmet, Kevlar:
NA($200-500) 1-5 units weight

Helmet, Metal:
5EP-1MP($500-5K) 6-20 units weight

Helmet, Plastic:
NA($50-200) 1-5 units weight

Hood, Chainmail:
1EP-5EP($125-500) 4-6 units weight

Jerkin, Hardened Leather:
5GP-1EP($250-500) 5 units weight

Jerkin, Hardened Leather w/ Metal Plate:
5EP-1PP($1K-3K) 30 units weight

Jerkin, Hardened Leather w/ Metal Studs:
5EP-8EP($1k-2K) 15 units weight

Jerkin, Hardened Leather w/ Sleeves:
5GP-1EP+1GP($250-500 + $50) 6 units weight

Jerkin, Hardened Leather w/ Wood Plate:
1EP-5EP($500-1K) 8 units weight

Jerkin, Leather, Sleeveless:
1GP-5GP($100-300) 3 units weight

Pants, Chainmail
1EP-5EP($1K-3K) 15 units weight

Pants, Hardened Leather:
1GP-5GP($250-500) 4 units weight

Pants, Hardened Leather w/ Metal Plate:
5EP-1PP($1K-3K) 20 units weight

Pants, Hardened Leather w/ Metal Studs:
1EP-3EP($800-2K) 12 units weight

Pants, Hardened Leather w/ Wood Plate:
5GP-1EP($500-1K) 8 units weight

Shield, Kevlar:
NA($450-600) 4-10 units weight

Shield, Plastic:
NA($50-350) 4-10 units weight

Shield, Wood or Metal:
1GP-1PP($50-3K) 4-40 units weight

Shin Guards, Metal:
1EP-5EP($75-200) 3 units weight/each

Shin Guards, Plastic:
NA($15-25) .5 unit weight/each

Shirt, Chainmail, Long-Sleeved:
1PP-5PP +1PP($1K-5K + $500) 24 units weight

Shirt, Chainmail, Short-Sleeved:
1PP-5PP($1K-5K) 20 units weight

Skirt, Hardened Leather:
1GP-5GP($125-500) 5-8 units weight

Thigh Guards, Metal:
1EP-5EP($125-500) 3 units weight/each

Thigh Guards, Plastic:
NA($15-25) .5 unit weight/each

Undercoat, Padded Fabric:
1SP-5SP($35-75) 2 units weight

Vest, Flak:
NA($300-500) 8 units weight

Vest, Kevlar:
NA($500-1K) 2 units weight

Wrist Guards, Metal:
5SP-1GP($15-500) 1 unit weight/each

CLOTHING

Belt:
3CP-1SP($5-50) .3 unit weight

Boots, Ankle-High, Soft Leather:
1SP-5SP($25-75) .5 unit weight/pair

Boots, Knee-High, Soft Leather:
3SP-8SP($50-125) 1 unit weight/pair

Boots, Thigh-High, Soft Leather:
1GP-3GP($100-300) 3 units weight/pair

Bra:
NA($5-50) .2 unit weight

Cloak/Cape, Floor-Length, Light Fabric:
5SP-1GP($75-300) 10 units weight

Cloak/Cape, Floor-Length, Medium Fabric:
1GP-5GP($125-500) 20 units weight

Cloak/Cape, Floor-Length, Heavy Fabric:
5GP-5EP($200-1K) 40 units weight

Cloak/Cape, Waist-Length, Light Fabric:
1SP-5SP($50-125) 2 units weight

Cloak/Cape, Waist-Length, Heavy Fabric:
5SP-1GP($75-300) 4 units weight

Dress (Style Varies):
1**SP**+($10+) 2 units weight+

Gloves, Fabric:
1**SP**-5**SP**($5-35) .6 unit weight/pair

Gloves, Leather:
5**SP**-5**GP**($35-125) .8 unit weight/pair

Handkerchief, Cotton:
2**CP**-1**SP**($1-5) .2 unit weight

Handkerchief, Silk:
1**SP**-1**GP**($10-25) .1 unit weight

Hat:
5**CP**-5**GP**($3-125) 1-5 units weight

Hose:
1**SP**-5**SP**($5-15) .3 unit weight

Pants, Fabric:
1**SP**-5**SP**($15-75) 1 unit weight

Pants, Leather:
5**SP**-1**GP**($75-325) 2 units weight

Robe, Light:
1**SP**-5**SP**($15-50) 5 units weight

Robe, Medium:
5**SP**-1**GP**($35-100) 10 units weight

Robe, Heavy:
1**GP**-5**GP**($50-300) 15 units weight

Sandals:
5**CP**-1**SP**($5-15) .4 unit weight/pair

Shirt, Cotton:
2**CP**-1**SP**($5-30) .4 unit weight

Shirt, Silk:
5**SP**-1**GP**($20-50) .2 unit weight

Surcoat:
5**SP**-5**GP**(NA) .8 unit weight

Tie:
NA($5-50) .1 unit weight

Underwear:
2**CP**-5**CP**($2-5) .2 unit weight

Vest, Fabric:
2**CP**-1**SP**($5-75) .2 unit weight

Vest, Leather:
1**SP**-5**SP**($50-125) .8 unit weight

Wig:
5**SP**-5**GP**($15-200) 1 unit weight.

MISCELLANEOUS

Backpack, Small:
5**CP**-1**SP**($10-15) .5 unit weight
holds 20 units weight

Backpack, Large:
8**CP**-3**SP**($10-50) .5 unit weight,
holds 20 units weight

Ball stand/Crystal Ball:
7**CP**-1**EP**($5-500) .2-10 units weight

Bandage, Linen:
5**CP**-1**SP**($1-2) .1 unit weight per square foot

Bandolier, Bullet:
NA($10-15) .5 unit weight
holds 100 bullets

Bandolier, Knife:
1**SP**-5**SP**($35-75) .5 unit weight
holds 6 daggers

Basket, Reed, Small:
2**CP**-1**SP**($5-10) .2 unit weight,
holds 5 units weight

Basket, Reed, Medium:
5**CP**-3**SP**($8-12) .4 unit weight,
holds 10 units weight

Basket, Reed, Large:
1**SP**-5**SP**($10-20) .8 unit weight,
holds 15 units weight

^Batteries:
NA($2-5) .2 unit weight
2pk. will last 400 Moves (20 rounds)

Belt, Bullet:
NA($10-20) .5 unit weight,
holds 50 bullets

Belt Pouch, Small:
2**CP**-5**CP**($2-10) .5 unit weight
holds 3 units weight

Belt Pouch, Medium:
5**CP**-1**SP**($5-20) .8 unit weight,
holds 6 units weight

Belt Pouch, Large:
1**SP**-5**SP**($10-45)1 unit weight,
holds 10 units weight

Bit & Bridle:
1**GP**-5**GP**($50-125) 2 units weight

Blanket:
8**CP**-5**SP**($10-25) 2 units weight

Blanket, Saddle:
1**SP**-5**SP**($50-125) 3 units weight

Boat, Small:
5**GP**-10**GP**($200-500) 50 units weight, 10'-15' long

Boat, Medium:
10**GP**-5**EP**($800-3K) 80 units weight, 15'-25' long

Boat, Large:
5**EP**-1**PP**($3K-15K) 125 units weight 25'-35' long

Book (300 pages):
1**GP**-20**GP**($1-15) 2.5 units weight, leather-bound

Book Pouch:
1**SP**-1**GP**($15-25) .5 unit weight

Bottle, Bone:
1**SP**-5**SP**($10-100) .2 unit weight

Bottle, Glass:
(see Specialty Weapon list)

Bottle of Ink:
1**SP**-2**GP**($1-5) .1 empty, .6 full (5 fluid ounces)

Bow String, Gut (Nylon):
0-2**CP**($1-3) .01 unit weight

Candle:
1**CP**-5**CP**($1-5) .1 unit weight, Lasts 100 Moves (5 rounds)

^Canteen:
NA($10-15) .2 empty, .8 full (5 fluid ounces)

Carriage, Small:
5**EP**-2**PP**($2000-5000) 100 units weight, Holds 600 unit weights (1 horse pulling)

Carriage, Medium:
2**PP**-1**MP**($5000-10000) 150 units weight, Holds 1000 unit weights (2 horses pulling)

Carriage, Large:
8**PP**-5**MP**($10000-15000) 200 units weight, Holds 3000 unit weights (4 horses pulling)

Chalk, Chunk (Stick):
0-5**CP**($.10-.50) .01 unit weight

^Chemical light:
NA($2-5) .2 unit weight, Lasts 100 Moves (5 rounds)

Cloth, Oil:
1**CP**-5**CP**($1-2) per square foot, .1 unit weight, waterproof

Cloth, Soft:
1**CP**-2**CP**($.25-1) per square foot/ .1 unit weight, useful for cleaning blades, etc.

Comb, Plastic:
NA($.50-1.50) .1 unit weight

Comb, Wood:
5**CP**-1**SP**($3-5) .1 unit weight

Crowbar:
2**SP**-5**SP**($5-10) 2 units weight, 1'6" damage as Metal Pipe

Crystal Ball, 2" Sphere:
1**SP**-5**SP**($10-20) .5 unit weight

Crystal Ball, 4" Sphere:
5**SP**-1**GP**($20-50) 1 unit weight

Crystal Ball, 6" Sphere:
1**GP**-5**GP**($50-100) 5 units weight

Crystal Ball, 12" Sphere:
1**EP**-1**PP**($250-500) 20 units weight

Curry Comb:
1**SP**-3**SP**($25-50) .5 unit weight, For horse grooming

Dart Case:
1**SP**-3**SP**($5-30) .5 unit weight, Holds 6 darts

Eye Liner, Kohl Stick (Pencil):
1**GP**-5**GP**($1-5) .1 unit weight

Eye Shadow, Pat (1 color):
1**GP**-5**GP**($2-5) .1 unit weight

^Flashlight:
NA($2-20) .2 to 2 units weight, Needs batteries to operate

Flask of Oil:
1**SP**-1**GP**($5-$10) .1 empty, .9 full (8 fluid ounces), Lasts 400 Moves (20 rounds)

Garden Tool, Shovel/Claw:
5**SP**-3**GP**($10-30) 2 units weight per set, shovel/claw 1'. Damage from shovel as **Katar**. Damage from Claw as **Hand Claws**

Gauze:
1**SP**-1**GP**($2-5) .3 unit weight per 100' roll 3" wide

Gunpowder:
1SP-1GP($1-5) .1 unit weight

Grappling Hook:
5SP-1GP($15-30) 3 units weight
Needs rope. Damage as **Hand Claws**

Hair Brush, Plastic w/ Plastic Bristle:
NA($5-10) .1 unit weight

Hair Brush, Wood w/ Boar Bristle:
1SP-1GP(NA) .1 unit weight

Hair Coloring:
1GP-5GP($5-10) .4 unit weight,
Lasts two weeks

Hammer:
1SP-5SP($5-10) 2 units weight,
1'. Damage as **War Hammer 1d8**

^Holster, Gun:
NA($15-200) .3 unit weight

Horseshoe:
1SP-2SP($5-10) 1 unit weight, Need 4

Incense Burner, Brass:
3SP-1GP($1-10) 2 unit weight

Lantern:
15SP-5GP($15-30) 1.5 units weight,
Needs fuel to operate

Lantern, Bullseye:
5GP-15GP($30-80) 2 units weight,
Needs fuel to operate

Lockpick, Advanced:
NA(NA)1000cr-5000cr .5 unit weight,
Will pick futuristic locks

Lockpick, Electronic:
NA($500-2000) 1 unit weight,
Will pick electronic locks

Lockpick, Modern:
NA($200-500) .5 unit weight,
Will pick modern locks

Lockpick, Old Style:
1EP.(NA) 1.5 units weight,
Will pick locks made up to 1900's

Map Case:
5SP-1GP($1-20) .5 unit weight,
Used for paper storage

Match:
1BR-5BR($.01) .01 unit weight,
Lasts 2 Moves

Mortar/Pestle, Ceramic:
1SP-1GP($15-25) .5 unit weight

Mortar/Pestle, Stone:
5SP-5GP($20-75) 1 unit weight

Needle, Silver, Stainless:
1SP-5SP($.10-1) .01 unit weight

Oars, Boat:
5SP-5GP($50-300) 3-20 units weight

Paper/Parchment:
5CP-1SP($.01-.05) .01 unit weight
per sheet of 8.5"x11"

Paint, Tube/Pat:
2SP-5SP($1-15) .2 unit weight

Paint Brush:
1SP-2SP($1-15) .2 unit weight

^Pen/Pencil:
(see Specialty weapons list)

Pipe (Smoking):
1CP-1GP($5-300) .3 unit weight,
Needs tobacco to use

Pocket Mirror, Silver:
1GP-1EP($1-5) .5 unit weight, 4"

Polish Stone:
0CP-5CP($0-5) .2 unit weight,
Used to polish blades

Powder Horn:
1SP-1GP($50-125) .2 unit weight empty
(holds .8 unit weight)

Prism, Glass:
1SP-1GP($5-10) .2 unit weight

Quarrel Case, Small:
1SP-4SP($30-75) .8 unit weight,
Holds 1 dozen

Quarrel Case, Medium:
4SP-8SP($45-100) 1.2 units weight,
Holds 2 dozen

Quarrel Case, Large:
1GP-5GP($75-200) 1.6 units weight,
Holds 3 dozen

Quill Pen:
0-**2CP**($1) .01 unit weight,
For writing, needs ink

Quiver, Small:
5CP-2SP($30-75) .5 unit weight,
Holds 1 dozen

Quiver, Medium:
1**SP**-5**SP**($50-100) .8 unit weight,
Holds 2 dozen

Quiver, Large:
5**SP**-2**GP**($75-125) 1 unit weight,
Holds 3 dozen

Razor, Disposable:
NA($.10-.50) .1 unit weight (no damage)

Razor, Electric:
NA($5-15) .4 unit weight,
Needs batteries to run (no damage)

Razor, Straight:
1**SP**-1**GP**($5-10) .3 unit weight,
Damage as **Stiletto/slash**

Rope, Hemp, 50':
1**SP**-5**SP**($20-40) 3 units weight,
300 units weight maximum

Rope, Nylon, 50':
NA($15-30) 1 unit weight,
800 units weight maximum

Rope, Silk, 50':
1**GP**-12**GP**($75-125) .5 unit weight,
600 units weight maximum

Sack, Small:
2**CP**-5**CP**($5-12) .1 unit weight,
Holds 10 units weight

Sack, Medium:
5**CP**-1**SP**($10-15) .2 unit weight,
Holds 25 units weight

Sack, Large:
8**CP**-2**SP**($15-25) .5 unit weight ,
Holds 40 units weight

Saddle, Pack:
5**SP**-5**GP**($300-600) 10 units weight

Saddle, Riding:
1**GP**-10**GP**($400-800) 15 units weight

Saddle Bags, Small:
5**SP**-8**GP**($50-200) 2 units weight,
Holds 10 unit weights

Saddle Bags, Medium:
8**SP**-12**GP**($100-250) 4 units weight,
Holds 20 units weight

Saddle Bags, Large:
1**GP**-20**GP**($200-400) 6 units weight,
Holds 40 units weight

Sail, Ship:
5**GP**-10**GP**($500-2K) 20 units weight

Scabbard, Sword:
5**CP**-1**GP**($15-100) .3 unit weight

Scale/Weights, Small:
1**GP**-1**EP**($50-100) 10 units weight

Shadow Brush, Cotton (Foam):
5**CP**-1**SP**($.50-1) .01 unit weight

Sheath, Knife or Dagger:
2**CP**-5**SP**($1-50) .1 unit weight

Sheepskin:
1**SP**-5**SP**($15-25) .1 unit weight
per sheet of 9"x12"

Ship, Very Small:
5**PP**-1**MP**($15K-25K) 200 units weight,
40'- 60' long

Ship, Small:
1**MP**-5**MP**($25K-40K) 300 units weight,
65'- 80' long

Ship, Medium:
5**MP**-10**MP**($40K-$60K) 400 units weight,
85'-100' long

Ship, Large:
10**MP**-30**MP**($60K-90K) 800 units weight,
150'- 200' long

Shovel, Small:
10**SP**-5**GP**($15-45) 4 units weight,
3'/ folded 1'6", Damage as **Falchion**

Soap:
5**CP**-1**SP**($.50-2) 2 unit weight

Spike/Piton:
(see Specialty weapons list)

Spool of Thread, Mending:
5**CP**-1**SP**($.50-2) .2 unit weight

Tent, Small:
1**GP**-5**GP**($75-125) 8 units weight,
1 to 2 persons

Tent, Medium:
5**GP**-1**EP**($150-300) 10 units weight,
2 to 4 persons

Tent, Large:
1**EP**-5**EP**($200-400) 15 units weight,
4 to 8 persons

Tinder Box:
2**SP**-1**GP**($15-45) 1 unit weight, flint/steel/straw

Tobacco, Full Pouch:
0-1**GP**($5-50) .1 unit weight, .6 unit weight full pouch

Torch:
2**CP**-5**CP**($0-15) .2 unit weight, Lasts 200 Moves (10 rounds)

Wagon, Small:
5**GP**-10**GP**($400-1000) 80 units weight, Holds 800 unit weights (1 horse pulling)

Wagon, Medium:
10**GP**-5**EP**($1000-3000) 150 units weight, Holds 2000 unit weights (2 horses pulling)

Wagon, Large:
5**EP**-2**PP**($3000-8000) 300 units weight, Holds 4000 unit weights (4 horses pulling)

Water Skin:
5**CP**-1**SP**($10-15) .1 empty, .6 full (5 fluid ounces)

Whetstone:
1**SP**($5-15) .2 unit weight, Used to sharpen blades

Wooden Box, Small:
1**CP**-5**CP**($5-10) .4 unit weight, 4"x 6"x 4"

Wooden Box, Medium:
5**CP**-1**SP**($10-15) .8 unit weight, 6"x 12"x 4"

Wooden Box, Large:
1**SP**-5**SP**($15-40) 1.5 units weight, 12"x 24"x 6"

Wooden Chest, Small:
5**SP**-1**GP**($50-100) 5 units weight, 8"x 12"x 14"

Wooden Chest, Medium:
1**GP**-5**GP**($75-150) 10 units weight, 12"x 14"x 18"

Wooden Chest, Large:
5**GP**-1**EP**($100-225) 15 units weight, 14"x 18"x 24"

Wooden Trunk, Small:
1**EP**-5**EP**($75-150) 15 units weight, 16"x 18"x 24"

Wooden Trunk, Medium:
5**EP**-1**PP**($125-300) 20 units weight, 18"x 24"x 24"

Wooden Trunk, Large:
1**PP**-5**PP**($150-500) 30 units weight, 24"x 32"x 24"

AMMO

Arrows, Silver-Tipped:
1**GP**-5**GP**($25-75) 1 unit weight (+5% penetration)

Arrows, Steel-Tipped:
1**SP**-2**SP**($5-10) .4 unit weight (+5% penetration)

Arrows, Wooden:
0-3**CP**($1-5) .2 unit weight

Bandolier, Bullet:
NA($10-15) .5 unit weight, Holds 100 bullets

Belt, Bullet:
NA($10-20) .5 unit weight, Holds 50 bullets

Blaster Pack, Small:
NA(1K-2Kcr) .5 unit weight, Holds 6 charges

Blaster Pack, Large:
NA(1.5K-3Kcr) .8 unit weight, Holds 10 charges

Blaster Recharger:
NA(3K-4Kcr) 8 units weight, Requires electrical outlet

Bow String, Gut (Nylon):
0-2**CP**($1-3) .01 unit weight

Disrupter Pack, Small:
NA(1K-2Kcr) .4 unit weight, Holds 4 charges

Disrupter Pack, Large:
NA(3K-4Kcr) .8 unit weight, Holds 8 charges

Disrupter Recharger:
NA(4K-8Kcr) 10 units weight, Requires electrical outlet

Flamer Fuel, Small:
NA(25-50cr/tank)

Flamer Fuel, Large:
NA(100-200cr/tank)

Flamer Tank, Small:
NA(100-200cr) 1 unit weight,
Holds 10 blasts

Flamer Tank, Large:
NA(300-500cr) 2 units weight,
Holds 20 blasts

Flintlock Ball, Iron/Steel:
5SP-1GP($50-100) .4 unit weight

Flintlock Ball, Silver:
1GP-5GP($150-300) .6 unit weight

Gunpowder:
1SP-1GP($1-5) .1 unit weight

Laser Pack, Small:
NA(100-300cr) .2 unit weight,
Holds 4 charges

Laser Pack, Large:
NA(300-600cr) .4 unit weight,
Holds 8 charges

Laser Recharger:
NA(500-1.5Kcr) 2 units weight,
Requires electrical outlet

Musket Ball, Iron/Steel:
1SP-5SP($15-35) .5 unit weight

Musket Ball, Silver:
1GP-5GP($75-125) .8 unit weight

Needle Clip, Small:
NA(100-300cr) .4 unit weight,
Holds 4 bursts

Needle Clip, Large:
NA(150-350cr) .6 unit weight,
Holds 6 bursts

Neuro Crossbow Clip:
NA(200-500cr) .5 unit weight,
Holds 6 charges

Phaser Pack, Small:
NA(2k-4Kcr) .5 unit weight,
Holds 12 charges

Phaser Pack, Large:
NA(4K-6Kcr) 1 unit weight,
Holds 24 charges

Phaser Recharger:
NA(3K-4Kcr) 5 units weight,
Requires electrical outlet

Photon Crossbow Clip:
NA(500-1Kcr) .1 unit weight,
Holds 2 charges

Photon Pack, Small:
NA(500-1Kcr) .4 unit weight,
Holds 6 charges

Photon Pack, Large:
NA(1K-2Kcr) .8 unit weight,
Holds 12 charges

Photon Recharger:
NA(1K-2Kcr) 5 units weight,
Requires electrical outlet

Pistol Ball, Iron/Steel:
5CP-1SP($10-20) .2 unit weight

Pistol Ball, Silver:
5SP-1GP($50-100) .4 unit weight

Pistol Rocket:
NA(100-200cr) .2 unit weight

Pistol Rocket Clip, Small:
NA(50-75cr) .2 unit weight,
Holds 2 Rockets

Pistol Rocket Clip, Large:
NA(100-200cr) .4 unit weight,
Holds 4 Rockets

Plasma Fuel, Small:
NA(500-1Kcr)

Plasma Fuel, Large:
NA(1K-3Kcr)

Plasma Crossbow Clip:
NA(500-1Kcr) .2 unit weight,
Holds 3 charges

Plasma Tank, Small:
NA(2K-4Kcr) 1 unit weight,
Holds 10 blasts

Plasma Tank, Large:
NA(3K-5Kcr) 2 units weight,
Holds 20 blasts

Powder Horn:
1SP-1GP($50-125) .2 unit weight empty
(holds .8 unit weight)

Quarrels, Silver-Tipped:
1GP-5GP($25-75) 1 unit weight
(+5% penetration)

Quarrels, Steel-Tipped:
1SP-2SP($5-10) .4 unit weight
(+5% penetration)

Quarrels, Wooden:
0-3**CP**($1-5) .2 unit weight

Sling Stones, Iron(Steel):
2**CP**-5**CP**($.50-1) .1 unit weight

Sling Stones, Silver:
1**SP**-5**SP**($4-8) .3 unit weight

Sonic Charge Pack, Small:
NA(100-300cr) .4 unit weight,
Holds 5 charges

Sonic Charge Pack, Large:
NA(200-600cr) .8 unit weight,
Holds 10 charges

Sonic Recharger:
NA(500-1.5Kcr) 2 units weight,
Requires electrical outlet

Tangle Clip, Small:
NA(75-125cr) .4 unit weight,
Holds 2 nets

Tangle Clip, Large:
NA(300-500cr) 1.2 units weight,
Holds 6 nets

Taser Clip, Small:
NA(25-75cr) .1 unit weight,
Holds 1 barb

Taser Clip, Large:
NA(100-200cr) .3 unit weight,
Holds 3 barbs

Taser Crossbow Clip:
NA(200-400cr) .4 unit weight,
Holds 12 charges

12 Gauge Shotgun Shell, Iron/Steel Shot:
NA($.75-1.25) .2 unit weight

12 Gauge Shotgun Shell, Silver Shot:
NA($5-10) .5 unit weight

12 Gauge Shotgun Shell, Wood Shot:
NA($1-2) .1 unit weight

.22 cal. Bullet:
NA($.10-.25) .01 unit weight

.22 cal. Bullet, Armor Piercing:
NA($.50-1) .01 unit weight

.22 cal. Bullet, Hollow Point:
NA($.50-1) .01 unit weight

.22 cal. Bullet, Silver:
NA($1-5) .05 unit weight

.22 cal. Bullet, Wood Core:
NA($.50-1) .01 unit weight

.32 cal. Bullet:
NA($.15-.30) .02 unit weight

.32 cal. Bullet, Armor Piercing:
NA($1-5) .05 unit weight

.32 cal. Bullet, Hollow Point:
NA($.50-1) .01 unit weight

.32 cal. Bullet, Silver:
NA($1-5) .05 unit weight

.32 cal. Bullet, Wood Core:
NA($.50-1) .01 unit weight

.45 cal. Bullet: NA($.25-1)
.05 unit weight

.45 cal. Bullet, Armor Piercing:
NA($2-8) .1 unit weight

.45 cal. Bullet, Hollow Point:
NA($1-5) .02 unit weight

.45 cal. Bullet, Silver:
NA($2-8).1 unit weight

.45 cal Bullet, Wood Core:
NA($.75-1.25) .02 unit weight

.50 cal Bullet:
NA($.75-1) .2 unit weigh

.50 cal Bullet, Armor Piercing:
NA($5-10) .4 unit weight

.50 cal Bullet, Hollow Point:
NA($2-8) .1 unit weight

.50 cal Bullet, Silver:
NA($5-10) .4 unit weight

.50 cal Bullet, Wood Core:
NA($1-5) .1 unit weight

5.56mm Bullet:
NA($.25-1) .05 unit weight

5.56mm Bullet, Armor Piercing:
NA($2-10) .1 unit weight

5.56mm Bullet, Hollow Point:
NA($1-5) .02 unit weight

5.56mm Bullet, Silver:
NA($2-10) .1 unit weight

5.56mm Bullet, Wood Core:
NA($.75-1.25) .05 unit weight

7.62mm Bullet:
NA($.50-1) .1 unit weight

7.62mm Bullet, Armor Piercing:
NA($5-10) .2 unit weight

7.62mm Bullet:, Hollow Point:
NA($1-5) .05 unit weight

7.62mm Bullet:, Silver:
NA($5-10) .2 unit weight

7.62mm Bullet, Wood Core:
NA($1-5) .05 unit weight

9mm Bullet:
NA($.20-.75) .02 unit weight

9mm Bullet, Armor Piercing:
NA($.20-.75) .02 unit weight

9mm Bullet, Hollow Point:
NA($1-5) .02 unit weight

9mm Bullet, Silver:
NA($2-8) .1 unit weight

9mm Bullet, Wood Core:
NA($.50-1) .01 unit weight

FOOD

Ale (10 oz. bottle):
5**CP**-1**PP**($2-500) 1.2 units weight

Apple:
0-1**CP**($.50-1) .3 unit weight

Bread:
1**CP**.($.05-.25) .01 unit weight per slice (10 per loaf)

Butter, Stick:
5**CP**-1**SP**($1-2) .2 unit weight

Carrot:
0-1**CP**($.50-1) .2 unit weight

Celery, Stalk:
0-1**CP**($.50-1) .2 unit weight

Cheese, Stick:
5**CP**-1**SP**($3-5) .5 unit weight

Corn, Ear:
0-3**CP**($.50-1) .2 unit weight

Grain (50 oz. bag):
0-1**SP**($5-15) 5 units weight

Lettuce, Head:
0-3**CP**($1-1.50) .5 unit weight

Meat Strip, Dried:
1**CP**-5**CP**($.50-1) .01 unit weight

Nuts (pk.):
0-5**CP**($.50-1) .1 unit weight, 20 nuts per pack

Oats (50 oz. bag):
0-1**SP**($2-15) 5 units weight

Onion:
0-1**CP**($.50-1) .3 unit weight

Pepper (10 oz. bag):
0-5**CP**($1-5) 1 unit weight

Potato:
0-2**CP**($.50-1) .3 unit weight

Rice (10 oz. bag):
0-1**SP**($2-5) 1 unit weight

Salt (10 oz. bag):
0-5**CP**($1-5) 1 unit weight

Sugar (10 oz. bag):
5**CP**-1**SP**($2-5) 1 unit weight

Travel Cake, Granola/Fruit:
1**CP**-5**CP**($1-2) .2 unit weight

Wine (10 oz. bottle):
1**SP**-1**PP**($5-500) 1.2 units weight

LIVESTOCK

Cat
0-1**SP**($0-300)

Cow
5**GP**+($500+)

Dog:
0-5**CP**($0-30)

Dog, Guard/War:
1**GP**+($200+)

Dog, Hunting:
1**SP**+($50+)

Goat:
5**SP**+($75+)

Hawk
1**GP**+($200+)

Horse, Pack:
10**GP**+($1K+)

Horse, Riding:
20**GP**+($1.5K+)

Horse, War:
50**GP**+($3K+)

Mule, Pack:
5**GP**+($300+)

Mule, Riding:
10**GP**+($500+)

Ox
5**GP**+($800+)

Pony, Riding:
10**GP**+($500+)

Pony, War:
25**GP**+($1k+)

Sheep
1**SP**+($75+)

LUXURIES

Beaver Fur Pelt:
1**GP**+($50+)

Beaver Fur Trim:
1**GP**+($50+)

Beaver Fur Cap/Jacket:
20**GP**+($100+)

Beaver Fur Coat:
100**GP**+($1K+)

Brocade:
(1-20**GP**($5-10) per square yard,
4 units weight.

Chinchilla Fur Pelt:
5**GP**+($100+)

Chinchilla Fur Trim:
10**GP**+($200+)

Chinchilla Fur Cap/Jacket:
50**GP**+($500+)

Chinchilla Fur Coat:
200**GP**+($2K+)

Ermine Fur Pelt:
4**GP**+($100+)

Ermine Fur Trim:
8**GP**+($150+)

Ermine Fur Cap/Jacket:
35**GP**+($400+)

Ermine Fur Coat:
150**GP**+($1K+)

Fox Fur Pelt:
5**GP**+($200+)

Fox Fur Trim:
10**GP**+($300+)

Fox Fur Cap/Jacket:
50**GP**+($500+)

Fox Fur Coat:
200**GP**+($2K+)

Incense:
(5**SP**-5**GP**($.50-2) per stick/cone,
.01 unit weight

Ivory:
(1**GP**-10**GP**($10-50) per unit of weight

Leopard Fur Pelt:
10**GP**+($1K+)

Leopard Fur Trim:
25**GP**+($500+)

Leopard Fur Cap/Jacket:
150**GP**+($1K+)

Leopard Fur Coat:
500**GP**+($5K+)

Mink Fur Pelt:
8**GP**+($500+)

Mink Fur Trim:
12**GP**+($500+)

Mink Fur Cap/Jacket:
100**GP**+($1K+)

Mink Fur Coat:
300**GP**+($3K+)

Oil, Scented:
(1-10**GP**($5-50) per ounce

Perfume:
(1-20**GP**($10-50) per ounce

Silk:
(1-10**GP**($5-10) per square yard,
.5 units weight

Tapestry:
(10-50**GP**($10-15) per square yard,
6 units weight

Wolf Fur Pelt:
2**GP**($200+)

Wolf Fur Trim:
4**GP**+($500+)

Wolf Fur Cap/Jacket:
50**GP**+($1K+)

Wolf Fur Coat:
150**GP**+($3K+)

LAND VEHICLES

(Generic 1900- 2000 A.D.)

Note: *Specific vehicles may be used: i.e., "Nissan Sentra," "Ford Ranger," etc., but their stats must be approved by the* **GM**.

Maneuverability rating adds or subtracts from a Character's ability to operate the vehicle at high speed or in complicated maneuvers (-10% for every pt. below 5, +5% for every point above 5). Also, some maneuvers require a certain maneuverability rating even to be possible; in these cases, there is a -20% for every point below the required level.

Bicycle: ($50-500)
0-30 mph (10 Moves), 60 mph maximum, 75 units weight, 1 seat, 500 units Carry-Weight maximum, Mileage NA, Cross Country, Maneuverable 8

Mini Van: ($20K-40K)
0-60mph (8 Moves), 120 mph maximum, 6000 units weight, 6 seats, 3500 units Carry-Weight maximum, 20 gal. gasoline w/ 30 miles per gal., Maneuverable 4

Moped: ($1K-5K)
0-40 mph (6 Moves), 60 mph maximum, 250 units weight, 1 seat, 500 units Carry-Weight maximum, 8 gal. gasoline w/ 35 miles per gal., Maneuverable 6

Motorcycle, Off-Road: ($3K-10K)
0-60 mph (6 Moves), 120 mph maximum, 400 units weight, 1 seat, 800 units Carry-Weight maximum, 10 gal. gasoline w/ 32 miles per gal., Cross Country, Maneuverable 8

Motorcycle, Street: ($5K-20K)
0-60 mph (6 Moves), 120 mph maximum, 1000 units weight, 2 seats, 1000 units Carry-Weight maximum, 15 gal. gasoline w/ 30 miles per gal., Maneuverable 7

Roller Blades: ($100-300)
0-40 mph (6 Moves), 60 mph maximum, 4 units weight per pair, 1 person, 350 units Carry-Weight maximum, Mileage NA, Maneuverable 7

Roller Skates: ($20-50)
0-30 mph (10 Move), 50 mph maximum, 4 units weight per pair, 1 person, 300 units Carry-Weight maximum, Mileage NA, Maneuverable 6

Skateboard: ($25-200)
0-30 mph (8 Moves), 50 mph maximum, 3 units weight, 1 person, 300 units Carry-Weight maximum, Mileage NA, Maneuverable 7

Snowmobile: ($5K-20K)
0-60 mph (6 Moves), 100 mph maximum, 500 units weight, 2 seats, 1000 units Carry-Weight maximum, 12 gal. gasoline w/ 25 miles per gal., Snow Only, Maneuverable 7

Turbo/2-Door: ($30K-80K)
0-60 mph (4 Moves), 400 mph maximum, 4500 units weight, 2 seats, 1500 units Carry-Weight maximum, 12 gal. gasoline w/ 40 miles per gal., Maneuverable 5

Turbo/4-Door: ($40K-100K)
0-60 mph (6 Moves), 350 mph maximum, 5000 units weight, 4 seats, 2500 units Carry-Weight maximum, 15 gal. gasoline w/ 35 miles per gal., Maneuverable 5

Van: ($30K-60K)
0-60 mph (12 Moves), 100 mph maximum, 6000 units weight, 8 seats, 5000 units Carry-Weight maximum, 30 gal. gasoline w/ 25 miles per gal., Maneuverable 3

V6 Engine/2-Door: ($10K-20K)
0-60 mph (6 Moves), 150 mph maximum, 4000 units weight, 2 seats, 1500 units Carry-Weight maximum, 10 gal. gasoline w/ 35 miles per gal., Maneuverable 5

V6 Engine/4-Door: ($15K-30K)
0-60 mph (8 Moves), 120 mph maximum, 4500 units weight, 4 seats, 2500 units Carry-Weight maximum, 14 gal. gasoline w/ 30 miles per gal., Maneuverable 5

V8 Engine/2-Door: ($20K-50K)
0-60 mph (5 Moves), 220 mph maximum, 4500 units weight, 4 seats, 2500 units Carry-Weight maximum, 14 gal. gasoline w/ 32 miles per gal., Maneuverable 6

V8 Engine/4-Door: ($20K-50K)
0-60 mph (6 Moves), 200 mph maximum, 5000 units weight, 4 seats, 3000 units Carry-Weight maximum, 15 gal. gasoline w/ 30 miles per gal., Maneuverable 6

4 x 4/V8/2-Door: ($25K-40K)
0-60 mph (5 Moves), 150 mph maximum, 4000 units weight, 4 seats, 2500 units Carry-Weight maximum, 14 gal. gasoline w/ 30 miles per gal., Cross Country, Maneuverable 7

4 x 4/V8/4-Door: ($35K-80K)
0-60 mph (8 Moves), 120 mph maximum, 5000 units weight, 6 seats, 4000 units Carry-Weight maximum, 20 gal. w/ 30 miles per gal., Cross Country, Maneuverable 6

AIR VEHICLES

Jet Plane, Cargo: ($2M-5M)
0-120 mph (20 Moves), 600 mph maximum, 150K units weight, seating varies, 300K units Carry-Weight maximum, 100K units weight jet fuel w/ 500 miles per 100 units weight, 1.5 miles runway, Maneuverable 3, 169' long/160' wingspan/40' height

Jet Plane, Fighter: ($1M-5M)
0-120 mph (10 Moves), 1200 mph maximum, 8K units weight, 2 seats, 15K units Carry-Weight maximum, 5K units weight jet fuel w/ 500 miles per 50 units weight, VTOL, Maneuverable 8, 40' long/35' wingspan/15' height

Jet Plane, Passenger: ($5M-10M)
0-120 mph (25 Moves), 600 mph maximum, 169K units weight, 120 seats, 350K units Carry-Weight maximum, 100K units weight jet fuel w/ 500 miles per 100 units weight, .75 mile runway, Maneuverable 4, 154' long/144' wingspan/52' height

Jet Plane, Private: ($250K-1M)
0-120 mph (15 Moves), 550 mph maximum, 10K units weight, 6 seats, 20K units Carry-Weight maximum, 5K units weight jet fuel w/ 500 miles per 50 units weight, .5 mile runway, Maneuverable 6, 65' long/60' wingspan/20' height

Helicopter, Assault: ($80K-200K),
0-120 mph (6 Moves), 200 mph maximum, 1000 units weight, 4 seats, 2700 units Carry-Weight maximum, 700 units weight airplane fuel w/ 200 miles per 10 units weight, VTOL, Maneuverable 9, 49' long/48' rotor diameter/10' height

Helicopter, Scout: ($200K-500K)
0-120 mph (6 Moves), 250 mph maximum, 2300 units weight, 6 seats, 4000 units Carry-Weight maximum, 1000 units weight airplane fuel w/ 100m/10 units weight, VTOL, Maneuverable 8, 42' long/ 37' rotor diameter/11' height

Helicopter, Transport: ($500K-2M)
0-100 mph (8 Moves), 200 mph maximum, 3000 units weight, 12 seats, 8000 units Carry-Weight maximum, 1500 units weight airplane fuel w/ 100 miles per 10 units weight, VTOL, Maneuverable 6, 72' long/52' rotor diameter/14' height.

WATER VEHICLES

Jet Ski: ($1K-2K)
0-60 mph (6 Moves), 120 mph maximum, 200 units weight, 1 seat, 600 units Carry-Weight maximum, 15 gal. gasoline w/ 30 miles per gal., Maneuverable 9

Motor Boat, Day/ Pleasure: ($5K-10K)
0-80 mph (8 Moves), 120 mph maximum, 1000 units weight, 6 seats, 5000 units Carry-Weight maximum, 50 gal. gasoline w/ 50 miles per gal., Maneuverable 7, 17' long/ 12'width/8' height

Motor Boat, Speed: ($20-50K)
0-80 mph (5 Moves), 200 mph maximum, 800 units weight, 4 seats, 2000 units Carry-Weight maximum, 50 gal. gasoline w/ 80 miles per gal., Maneuverable 9, 24' long/8' width/6' height

Motor Boat, Yacht: ($80K-200K)
0-60 mph (7 Moves), 150 mph maximum, 2000 units weight, 8 seats, 6000 units Carry-Weight maximum, 100 gal. gasoline w/ 65 miles per gal., Maneuverable 8, 37' long/12' width/20' height, 4-person cabin

COMPUTER/CYBERLINK

Note: *Special Equipment must be approved by the **GM**. The "Data Web" supplement newsletter gives listings of specialized equipment for **GMs** and players who do not have the time to come up with rules for gadgets.*

Cyberdeck: (6K-12Kcr)
6MB program memory; Semsense and Virtual Reality Interface Filter; Data Web access cable, brain jack cable, and outlet cable included

Cyberlink Implant : (10K-14Kcr)
Generic link to cyberdecks and cyber rigs

Smartrig Cyberlink: (20K-30Kcr)
Turns vehicle into a cyber extension. All vehicle systems can be run by the Character with a cyberlink implant

CYBERDECK PROGRAMS

Note: *Programs cost 100cr per Megabyte (**MB**) + 50cr per Color Level upgrade, up to Orange 10. Programs above Orange 10 must be purchased at Black Market prices or created by the Character. There is an additional 1/2 **MB** for each color level upgrade plus 10cr per level number within the color grade.*

Sensor Attack: This program attacks the "Semsense" program of another "jacker" or the sensor programs of defense systems. The result makes the victim blind and deaf in the data web until the program is repaired. Can be styled by user. Takes 2 moves to run program

Sensor Swarm: This program creates a swarm of static spheres to surround and confuse enemy programs, other "jackers," techno-mages, etc. This program can be styled to appear as bubbles, colored rubber balls, butterflies, stars, birds, rabbits, spiders, or just about anything. Causes a 5-Move delay in victim's action. Takes 1 Move to run program

Color Levels

1) White (Levels 1 through 10)

2) Blue (Levels 1 through 10)

3) Green (Levels 1 through 10)

4) Yellow (Levels 1 through 10)

5) Orange (Levels 1 through 10)

6) Red (Levels 1 through 10)

7) Purple (Levels 1 through 10)

8) Black (Levels 1 through 10)

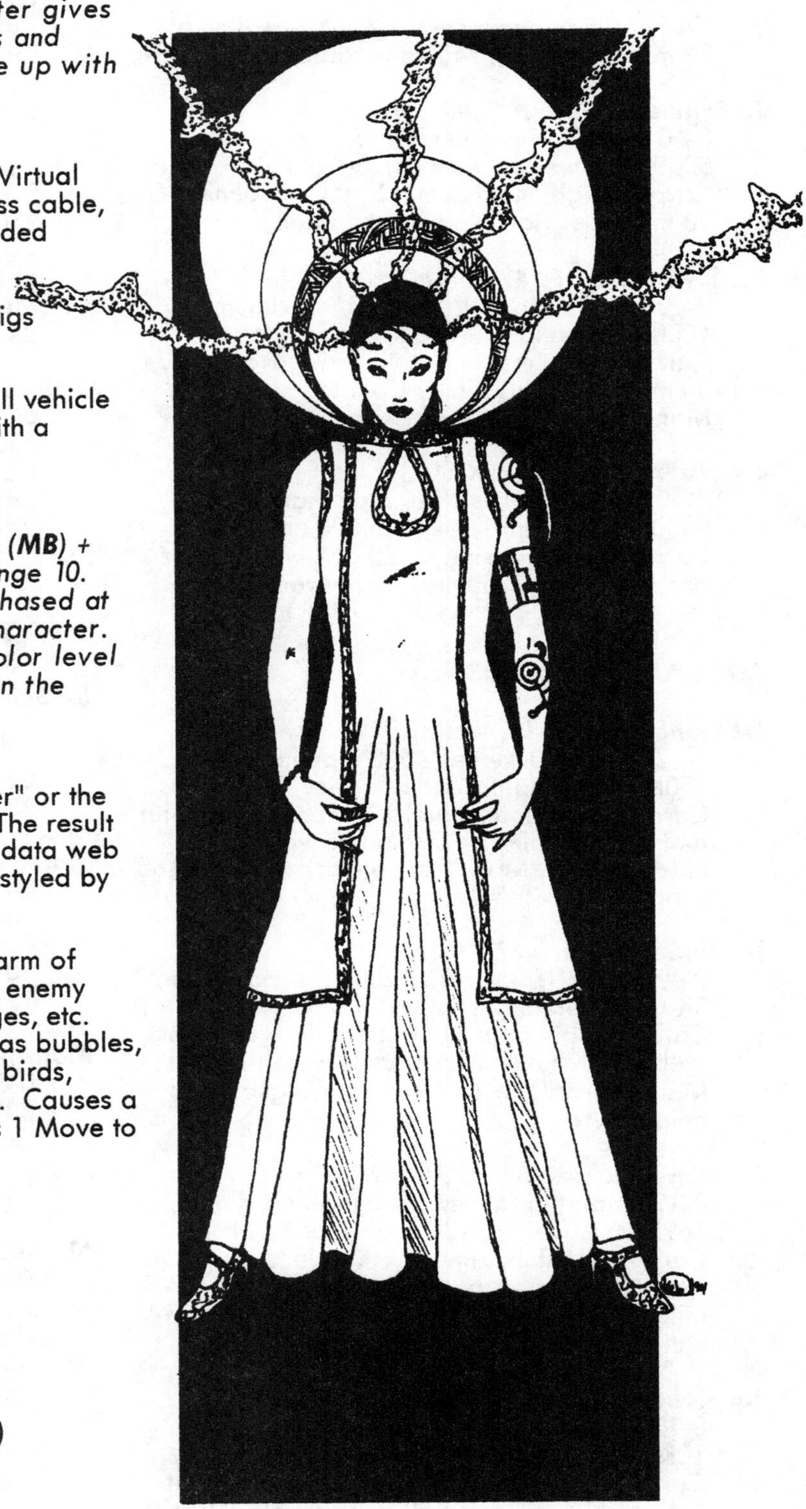

COMBAT OPERATION

If you are the *Gamemaster*, be sure to read and understand the Combat section fully. Combat can be easy or complex depending on how much detail you wish to get into. I tend to run the easier system. I stress the story and role playing more than the blood-and-guts detail of combat. Some **GMs** like to keep track of the players' injuries for them, telling them only that they are hurt badly or bleeding freely. This is preferable to saying "You're down 6 hit points." I mean, do *you* know how many hit points you have? It also tends to make players more cautious. However, it does make for extra bookwork for the **GM** (as if there isn't enough already).

Combat Movement

Combat is divided into a series of *Moves* enacted by each combatant. A *Combat Sequence* can sometimes be started by a *surprise attack*. Under this circumstance (and *only* this circumstance), the attacker has the advantage of surprise and gets a *free Move* which cannot be responded to by the victim.

The rest of a combat (or all of it, if no one is surprised) consists of *phases*. Each *phase* is actually *four Combat Sequences*, at the end of which each Character will lose 2 **END** points. When your Character runs out of **END** points, you areno longer able to continue fighting.

Your Character's *Agility* (**AG**) is what determines how many Moves he/she can make in each *Combat Phase*. Your Character's **AG** must be equal to or more than the number listed in order to make that number of Moves.

For example, if your Character's **AG** is 43, your Character can make 3 Moves (1, 21, 41) for the *first Combat Sequence*. If your opponent has only an **AG** of 20, he can only make one Move (1) in the first *Combat Sequence*. As the *Combat Sequences* in each *phase* continue, your **AG** starts to wear a bit. Your Character can still enact three Moves in the second and third *Combat Sequences:* (2, 22, 42) and (3, 23, 43) respectively, but by the fourth *Combat Sequence* your Character is down to *two* Moves (4, 24). At this time your first *phase* is terminated, and your Character must deduct 2 points from his or her **END**.

By the beginning of *Phase 2*, your Character is now down to *two* Moves per *Combat Sequence* and will continue this way until the end of *Phase 5*.

If by some misbegotten chance your combat isn't completed by the end of *Phase 5*, you begin at the beginning of *Phase 1* again, in which case your Character has three Moves per *Combat Sequence* again . . . and thus it continues until you run out of **END** or the combat ends.

Note: Some actions, such as *Dodge*, take only *half* a Move. Therefore, you can actually do *two Dodges* in one Move (see *Combat Actions* or the *Hand-to-Hand* and *Martial Arts* segments of the *Character Skills* sections of this manual for details).

Combat Segments

Phase 1	1	21	41	61	81	
	2	22	42	62	82	
	3	23	43	63	83	
	4	24	44	64	84	-2 **END**
Phase 2	5	25	45	65	85	
	6	26	46	66	86	
	7	27	47	67	87	
	8	28	48	68	88	-2 **END**
Phase 3	9	29	49	69	89	
	10	30	50	70	90	
	11	31	51	71	91	
	12	32	52	72	92	-2 **END**
Phase 4	13	33	53	73	93	
	14	34	54	74	94	
	15	35	55	75	95	
	16	36	56	76	96	-2 **END**
Phase 5	17	37	57	77	97	
	18	38	58	78	98	
	19	39	59	79	99	
	20	40	60	80	100	-2 **END**

COMBAT

Combat in **Webs** can be simple or complex, depending on what system your **GM** decides to use. All the combat systems require you to roll your skill percentage to use whatever attack you choose.

All systems operate on *Combat Segments* which determine who moves first by agility or surprise. The differences in the systems come in how hit locations are determined and how armor is used. Hit location charts and armor descriptions are given in this section. There is also an example of how to run combat.

A Character may not have better than 100 **AG** by *any* means magical or otherwise. A Character must check the chart to see how many Moves he/she will get in a particular phase. If a Character uses skills or magic to boost his/her speed the Character is committed to the required endurance loss.

Let's look at some common actions and how long they take.

Combat Actions

ANIMALS: **Bite** 1mv., **Claw** 1mv., **Tail Bash** 1 1/2mv., **Pounce** 2mv., **Dodge** 1/2mv., **Jump** 1mv., **Roll** 1mv., **Breath Attack** 1 1/2mv., **Natural Ability Attack** 1mv., **Turn** 1mv., **Pull Free** 2mv.

HUMANOIDS:(same as *Animals*) **Parry** 1mv., **Draw Weapon** 1 mv., **Load Weapon** 1mv., **Aim Weapon** 1mv., **Attack** 1mv./hand, **Walk MA** 1mv., **Drop Item** 1/2 mv., **Dive** 1mv., **Kick** 1 1/2mv., **Punch** 1 1/2mv., **Whisper/Yell**(2 words) 1/2mv., **Throw** 2mv., **Stand** 2mv., **Thrust** 1mv., **Lunge** 1 1/2mv., **Slash** 1 1/2mv., **Disarm** 2mv., **Grab** 1mv., **Shove** 1 1/2mv., **Pump Weapon** 1/2mv.

Certain skills or fighting techniques allow these moves to be made faster. *Hand-to-Hand* and *Martial Arts* maneuvers are listed and Specialty skills within these techniques are listed in following sections.

Combat Modifiers

Each Distraction -1%
Target Prone +5%
Attacker Prone -10%
Target Sitting/Kneeling +2%
Dim Light -10%
Attacking to Side -2%
Attacker Sitting/Kneeling -10%
Attacking from Side +5%
Attacking to Back -15%
Attacking from Back +15%
Attacking from Above +5%
Attacking from Below -2%
In Darkness/Blind -80%
Attacker Wounded -5%/pt of wound
Narrow Passage -20%
Wide Passage +0%
Each Obstacle -2%
Low Roof -10%
Turn in Passage -40%

Note: Not all modifiers will apply because of a Character's size, choice of weapon, etc. These listed above are simply guidelines.

Hand-to-Hand

The *HAND-to-HAND* skill allows a Character to buy the following Speciality skills:

HAYMAKER: (10**BP**, **STR**, 3**BP**/1pt., 2mv.) Doubles the normal damage of a Characters' hand attack.

TACKLE: (10**BP**, **STR**, 2**BP**/1pt., 2mv.) Does no damage but knocks a Character off his or her feet or mount.

HEAD BUTT: (5**BP**, **STR**, 2**BP**/1pt., 1mv.) Allows Character to use head as a weapon(1**d6** damage + **STR** bonus).

BOXING: (10**BP**, **STR**, 3**BP**/1pt.) Allows for a **cross** +2, **hook** +1 (1mv.), or **jab** (1/2mv.).

KIDNEY BLOW:(5**BP**, **AG**, 3**BP**/1pt.) An aimed blow that does +3 damage if properly done (this can also be used by Brawlers).

ROUNDHOUSE:(10**BP**, **STR**, 5**BP**/1pt., 3mvs.) Triples hand-attack damage.

BODY SLAM: (10**BP**, **STR**, 5**BP**/1pt., 3mvs.) Character bodily lifts and hurls victim to the ground. Victim is unable to move for 1 phase.

BREAK BONE: (10**BP**, **STR**, 5**BP**/1pt., 2mvs.) Character locks onto a victim's limb and drives knee into it. This maneuver must follow a successful **Wrist Grab/Lock**.

Martial Arts

The *MARTIAL ARTS* skill allows a Character to buy the following Speciality skills:

BACKWARD KICK: (10**BP**, **AG**, 3**BP**/1pt., 1mv.) Allows a Character to kick opponents who are behind without damage or hit penalties.

CIRCLE KICK: (10**BP**, **AG**, 3**BP**/1pt., 1 1/2mv.) A dramatic *Martial Arts* kick, where the Character builds up power by spinning in a complete circle before landing the kick. Does double damage if successful. If missed, Character loses 1mv. to recover.

DEFLECT/CATCH WEAPON: (30**BP**, **AG**, 5**BP**/1pt., 1/2 mv.) Can be used against missile weapons only. Allows the Character to deflect or catch thrown weapons directed at them. Can stop bullets, but Character is at a -50%.

FLYING KICK: (30**BP**, **AG**, 3**BP**/1pt., 2mv.) The Character leaps at the victim, leading with a powerful kick. The kick will do triple damage if it lands. If it fails, the Character will take 4mvs. to recover.

IRON CLAW: (30**BP**, **STR**, 1mv.) Allows the Character to develop immense crushing strength in his or her hands to shatter stone, snap/bend weapons, break bones, etc. Requires a successful **Wrist Grab/Lock**. Causes 1pt./time taken crushing damage (**STR** bonuses still apply), or the Character can crush 1/2" thickness/time taken of wood or bone, 1/4" thickness/time taken of stone or ice, and 1/8" thickness/time taken of metal.

IRON STRIKE: (30**BP**, **STR**, 1mv.) Is the same as **Iron Claw,** only is used as a side-of-hand chopping blow or punch rather than a crush. Does not require a grab to use.

IRON SKIN: (30**BP**) Allows Character to utilize his or her muscle density to increase resistance to weapon blows. Increases by 1 *Armor Class* (**AC**)/time taken to a maximum of 10.

NERVE STRIKE/PARALYZE: (30**BP**, **INT**, 5**BP**/1pt., 1mv.) Allows a Character to know where to apply pressure to a victim's nerve centers to paralyze him/her for one phase.

SUPER LEAP: (10**BP**) Allows a Character to make extraordinary leaps. From a standing start, the Character will be able to leap his or her height plus 1'/time taken forward and 1/2 his or her height + 1/2 foot/time taken upward. With a running start, the Character can double these distances.

WRIST GRAB/LOCK: (10**BP**, **AG**, 3**BP**/1pt., 1mv.) Allows the Character to incapacitate a Character by locking victim's in a painful hold. Unless the victim can ignore pain, he or she will not be able to continue the fight so long as the wrist is held.

CHOKE HOLD: (20**BP**, **AG**, 3**BP**/1pt., 3mv.) This maneuver allows the Character to grab and lock an opponent's throat in a hold until he or she passes out or dies.

BODY THROW: (see *Slam* under **Hand-to-Hand**)

LIGHTNING STRIKE: (30**BP**, **STR**, 5**BP**/1pt., 1mv.) Doubles damage from hand attacks.

DEATH BLOW: (30**BP**, **STR**, 5**BP**/1pt., 2mv.) Triples damage from hand attacks.

A *Gamemaster* may allow other specialized forms of *Martial Arts*. If they do check with them about other possible maneuvers. Game supplements for **Webs** will detail any such skills. Spells and psions take various Moves to accomplish according to the particular spell or psion used. These will be listed with the spell or psion and should be taken into consideration when planning attacks.

TAKING HITS

As with *Skills* acquisition, there are two *Combat* systems to choose from. The first is the simplest, the second, more involved. Feel free to choose whichever system you prefer, but be sure, as always, to remain consistent within your setup.

System 1: The Easy Way

In this system, the **GM** uses 1**d8** to determine where a Character is hit, the numbers being:

1. **Head**	4. **Right Arm**	7. **Torso**
2. **Torso**	5. **Left Leg**	8. **Head**
3. **Left Arm**	6. **Right Leg**	

System 2: The Nitpicker's Way

In this system, the rolls allow for more specific *Hit* locations. You first roll a 1**d8** to get the general location of the damage, and then roll another die for more specific information. The general rolls are identical to the other system, breaking down into:

1. **Head**	4. **Right Arm**	7. **Torso**
2. **Torso**	5. **Left Leg**	8. **Head**
3. **Left Arm**	6. **Right Leg**	

The secondary rolls are as follows:

HEAD: (1d6)

1. **Head**	4. **Right Eye**
2. **Neck**	5. **Temple, Left or Right**
3. **Left Eye**	6. **Back of Head**

Note: Areas **5** and **6** may not be possible from the Character's position, so only roll 1**d4** in such a circumstance. There is also a **50%** chance that any *Head Wound* is critical, and a **70%** chance that any *Critical Wound* will be an *Instant Death Wound*.

TORSO: (1d6)

1. **Chest**	4. **Groin**
2. **Left Side**	5. **Back**
3. **Right Side**	6. **Vital Organ**

Vital Organ, in turn, breaks down to (1**d4**):

1. **Heart**	3. **Kidney**
2. **Lung**	4. **Intestines**

Note: There is a **50%** chance that any vital organ hit is an *Instant Death Wound*.

ARM: (1d6)

1. **Hand**	3. **Forearm**	5. **Upper Arm**
2. **Wrist**	4. **Elbow**	6. **Shoulder**

Note: There is a **30%** chance that any *Arm Wound* will be critical, and a **40%** chance that any *Critical Wound* will result in amputation.

LEG: (1d6)

1. **Foot**	3. **Shin/Calf**	5. **Thigh**
2. **Ankle**	4. **Knee**	6. **Crippling Wound**

Note: There is a **30%** chance that any leg wound is a *Critical Wound*, and a **30%** chance that any *Critical Wound* will result in amputation. A *Crippling Wound* will render the leg useless even if it hasn't sustained a *Critical Wound*.

Hit Point Distribution

There are six major areas on the bodies of humanoid Characters which can take damage: **Head**, **Torso**, L/R **Arms**, L/R **Legs**. When setting up a Character, the player should distribute available *Hit Points* as evenly as possible among these areas. There must be at least one point for each area. If an area is reduced to 0 hit points, that area of the Character's body can no longer be used. **Head** reduced to 0 means that a Character is unconscious, and **Torso** at 0 means the Character is paralyzed and unable to fight. We strongly recommend you put extra points into **Torso** and **Head,** since these are the major targets.

ARMOR

In **System 1: The Easy Way**, only a general *Armor Class* (**AC**) is necessary for each location on a Character's body. In **System 2: The Nitpicker's Way**, you will need to list *what* type of Armor and what **AC** each is for all possible target areas.

Armor Classes

0 No armor, bare skin or light fabrics
1 Medium weight or padded fabrics
2 Heavy fabrics
3 Soft leathers
4 Medium-weight leather or padded soft leather. Reed or Bamboo Armor
5 Heavy leather, soft leather with shell or wood stud
6 Hardened leather, soft leather with metal studs
7 Light-chain, wood or shell-scale armor, plastic
8 Chainmail, scale mail, wooden plate
9 Light-chain mail with partial plate, Elvin light chain
10 Plate mail, scale mail over light-chain, Elvin chain
11 Drake or Wyvern hide, elvin light-chain, and partial plate
12 Young Wyrm, Moat Turtle, or Hydra hide, Elvin plate
13+ Various mythic beast hides, Magical armors, high-tech metals

AN EXAMPLE OF COMBAT

Let's say the Thief Tika is fighting a Goblin named Grog. Tika is a *Player Character*, whereas the Goblin is a *Non-Player Character* being operated by the **GM**.

Tika has an *Agility* of 25 and Grog has 20. Normally Tika, being faster, would move first, but this time Grog has set an ambush and consequently gets one *free Move* for surprise. Tika will not get a chance to dodge this Move, since Grog has the surprise advantage.

Grog is a Knife Fighter, and has to get close to use his weapon. He is currently hiding in a tree, so he'll have to jump down to reach Tika, thus "jumping" is his *free Move*.

Fortunately for him, he lands on Tika. Grog wasn't very high up in the tree and isn't very heavy, so the **GM** decides that both Characters will only take **1d4** of damage when Grog lands on Tika.

Grog rolls a 2. Tika wears Medium-Weight Leather Armor (as does Grog) so has an *Armor Class* (**AC**) of 4. Two points of damage isn't enough to penetrate her armor, so she and the armor are unharmed.

She now has *first Move* because of her *Agility* (**AG**), and the first Combat phase begins. She checks the chart, and because of her 25 **AG,** she gets a **Move 21** first, then a **Move 1**.

She first attempts to *Fast Draw* her weapon (also a dagger). Her *Fast Draw* skill stands at 55%, and she rolls a 51 on her percentage dice. Therefore she can *Fast Draw* her dagger without wasting one of her Moves.

She "turns" on her **Move 21** (turning is a 1Move action) and "attacks" on her **Move 1** (since attacking is also a 1 Move action, she can complete both movements). She has 85% to hit with her dagger and rolls 46 (a hit if Grog doesn't dodge).

In this phase (**Phase 1**), Grog only has a **Move 1** and will use it to dodge. He knows his *Dagger Skill* is 95%, while his *Dodge/Parry Skill* is only 75%. Since Tika is using a dagger attack and *Dagger Skill* gives him -10% against another dagger user to dodge, he will use the higher score to roll against (95 - 10 = 85, which is better than 75).

Because Tika made her *To Hit* roll by 39% (figure 85 her dagger skill - 46 what she rolled = 39), Grog is at a -39% to dodge. Since 85 - 39 = 46, Grog must roll a 46 or less to dodge. He rolls a 53.

At this point the *Gamemaster* (**GM**) rolls for the location of the damage using one of the two *Systems* listed in this manual, in this case **System 1: The Easy Way**.

The **GM** rolls a 2, so Tika has hit Grog in the chest with her dagger. Tika now rolls her *Attack Damage*. Her dagger does 1**d10,** and she rolls a 9.

Having **AC**4, Grog only takes 5 points of damage to his **Torso**. He has 7 *Hit Points* in his **Torso** so he can still fight but is badly wounded. Naturally, this rather hurts, so he elects to scream in pain.

Grog's cry of alarm could be a potential problem for Tika. She checks the chart and sees that she has a **Move 22** and a **Move 2** available. Figuring there are probably other Goblins around, she has to finish this guy off fast.

She decides to make both of her Moves *dagger attacks*. She rolls a 72 and a 36, so both attacks are good. Grog can only dodge 1 of them. In this case, 85 Tika's skill - 72 her roll = 13, so Grog is at -13 to dodge and must roll 72 or less.

He rolls 61 and dodges the first attack. Unfortunately for him, he's obliged to take the second attack because he's out of moves.

The **GM** rolls another **Torso** hit. Since Grog's armor has already been depleted at that location, he'll have to take full damage.

Tika rolls a 5 on her attack. Grog only had 2 points left in his **Torso,** so his **Torso** is now at -3. He is no longer able to move and is bleeding to death.

At this moment, two more Goblins show up on the scene, drawn by Grog's cries of pain. Tika hears them coming, and can see that one's armed with a spear, the other with a dagger. She also knows she only has four more Moves in **Phase 1** (**24, 23, 3**, and **4**). The Goblins, on the other hand, are fresh to the fight and as a result may be faster than she is.

She checks her skills and finds she has *Running Sprint* at 75%. She uses her **Move 23** to turn and her **Move 3** to sprint away from the scene. She rolls a 52 and heads off at a tremendous rate of speed, the Goblins in hot pursuit.

This is the way Combat happens when it is broken down into rolls and percentages. The actual game play would normally sound more like this:

GM: "Tika is walking down the old forest trail toward home as the sun begins to set. The trees are thick and full of shadows; some of them stretch over the road."

Tika: "Okay, I move faster. I don't want to be out in the woods after dark. I'm a *Hafling* so I'll use my sensitive hearing and sense of smell to see if anything is near."

GM: (First checks to see if Grog makes his *Move Silently, Breathe Silently* rolls and checks wind direction. According to the rolls, Tika won't be able to hear or smell him.) "What's your *Perception Score, Tika?*"

Tika: "64%." (She rolls an 80.) "I failed it."

GM: "Fine. As you pass under a rather large oak, you feel a large object drop onto your back."

Tika: (Rolls for *Fast Draw* and makes it.) "I turn while quickly drawing my dagger (makes her *Hit Roll*) and stab at the object."

GM: (Fails Grog's *Dodge Roll*.) "Your blade bites deeply into the chest of a foul-smelling Goblin."

Tika: (Surprised) "How did my nose miss that?"

GM: "Wind was wrong, and he was up too high."

Tika: "Hmmm. Well, where there's one, there's bound to be more." (Rolls *To Hit* twice.) "I stab at him two more times."

GM: (Making the *Dodge Roll* for Grog) "Your first stab goes wild, but the second lands very near your first strike. The Goblin falls, leaking blood. You raise your head in time to see two more Goblins charge out of the undergrowth. One carries a spear, the other has a long dagger. The one with the dagger snarls at you."

Tika: "Okay, I turn and run (Makes her roll), sprinting for Brandy Town as fast as I can go."

GM: "With an ear-splitting screech, the Goblins charge after you."

As you can see, actual play is much more interesting than the specifics of who goes when or what number is rolled. Tika could have stayed to fight, but unless she could kill the other Goblins quickly, the odds would quickly have turned against her. At the end of the phase, Tika would have lost 2 Endurance points for the fight and another 2 for the Sprinting.

UNUSUAL COMBAT SITUATIONS

In certain environments, *Combat* can be a little trickier. In the *Astral Plane*, for instance, **STR** is determined by your **CNC**; **AG** by your **PCP**; and *Hit Points* by your **PSP + END**.

On the *Essence/Spirit Plane*, **STR** is the same as your **WILL**; **AG** is determined by your **CNC**; and *Hit points* by your **POWER + END**.

In the **Data Webs** of *Virtual Reality*, **STR** is the

same as your **WILL**; **AG** your **CNC**; and *Hit Points* your **END**.

The reason for these modifications in these situations is that on these planes of existence your Character has no physical form. Therefore, it is the power of the Character's *mind* and *spirit* which become important, and it is the Character's *mind* and/or *spirit* that takes the actual damage.

BESTIARY
(or a Beginner's List of Opponents)

Baboon

The Baboon is a large, herbivorous primate. They normally have brown or gray fur, long arms and legs, large heads with dog-like muzzles and sharp canine teeth. Some have tails. Baboons are territorial and will try to drive invaders off. Baboons have been known to hunt, but this is not a common behavior.

STR: 12 **AG**: 16 **INT**: 7 **WIS**: 7 **CH**: 6 **CON**: 12 **END**: 24 **WILL**: 14 **POWER**: NA **CC**: 140 units **MR**: 5 **Hit Points**: 12 - 24 max. **Size**: 3 - 4'
MA: 3'/48'/96'/24'
Attacks: Hands/Feet 1**d6**+3, Bite 1**d6**
CBP: 100 **AC**: 1

Badger

Badgers are nocturnal, carnivorous, burrowing animals. They are territorial and fearless--often attacking creatures much larger than themselves. Badgers will try to retreat if not near their burrow, but otherwise they will fight to the death.

STR: 8 **AG**: 20 **INT**: 4 **WIS**: 4 **CH**: 6 **CON**: 8 **END**: 20 **WILL**: 8 **POWER**: NA **CC**: 80 units **MR**: 8 **Hit Points**: 8 - 20 max. **Size**: 2'
MA: 2'/40'/80'/20'
Attacks: Claws 1**d6**, Bite 1**d6**
CBP: 100 **AC**:2

Bear

Bears come in a variety of types: Black, Brown, Cave, Gray, and Polar. Each bear has its own distinct characteristics.

Black Bear

Black Bears are one of the smaller species of bears. They are often found in woodlands and are not overly aggressive. They feed mostly on insects, small mammals, fruits, and nuts. They are curious animals and will often wander into campsites in search of food. Black Bears have a remarkable sense of smell to 120' and are rarely surprised.

STR: 18 **AG**: 20 **INT**: 6 **WIS**: 6 **CH**: 6 **CON**: 18 **END**: 36 **WILL**: 12 **POWER**: NA **CC**: 200 units **MR**: 10 **Hit Points**: 30 -100 max. **Size**: 4-6'
MA: 4'/80'/160'/40'
Attacks: Claws 1**d8**+2, Bite 1**d6**, Hug 1**d10** crushing
CBP: 1000 **AC**: 3

Brown Bear

Brown Bears are large, territorial, and aggressive. They are found in cooler climates, woodlands, plains, and mountains. They feed mostly on meat and will take down large prey such as Elk and Moose. They have a good sense of smell to 120', and can move silently when they wish.

STR: 25 **AG**: 22 **INT**: 7 **WIS**: 7 **CH**: 6 **CON**: 20 **END**: 45 **WILL**: 14 **POWER**: NA **CC**:300 units **MR**: 10 **Hit Points**: 40 - 120 max. **Size**: 8-12'
MA: 10'/220'/440'/110'
Attacks: Claws 1**d10**+6, Bite 1**d8**, Hug 2**d10** crushing
CBP: 4000 **AC**: 3

Cave Bear

Cave Bears are the biggest of the bear species. They are not overly aggressive, but will defend their territory against intruders. The canines of the Cave Bear are elongated for stabbing large prey. Cave Bears are found in colder climates and normally hunt only large game. They have a good sense of smell to 80', and can move silently when they wish.

STR: 40 **AG**: 20 **INT**: 6 **WIS**: 6 **CH**: 6 **CON**: 40 **END**: 80 **WILL**: 12 **POWER**: NA **CC**: 500 unit **MR**: 15 **Hit Points**: 60 - 200 max. **Size**: 12 -16'
MA: 12'/240'/480'/120'
Attacks: Claws 2**d10**+8, Bite **d10**+4, Hug 3**d10** crushing
CBP: 10000 **AC**: 4

Gray Bear

Gray Bears are the smallest of the common bear species. They are highly aggressive hunters and quite intelligent. Gray Bears are the only bear known to hunt in packs and are not afraid of attacking large prey. They are found almost exclusively in mountain woodlands and use natural traps (such as dead-end washes) to help capture prey.

STR: 12 **AG:** 30 **INT:** 9 **WIS:** 9 **CH:** 7 **CON:** 12
END: 24 **WILL:** 18 **POWER:** NA **CC:** 150 units
MR: 5 **Hit Points:** 20 - 60 max. **Size:** 3 - 4'
MA: 3'/90'/180'/45'
Attacks: Claws 1**d8**+2, Bite 1**d6**, Hug 1**d8** crushing
CBP: 1000 **AC:** 3

Polar Bear

Polar Bears are similar to Brown Bears in size and behavior. Most Polar Bears spend their lives on the northern and southern polar ice floes. They are strong swimmers and are well insulated against the cold. They eat fish and medium-sized mammals most of the time. They have little to no fear of humanoids and will consider them as prey if other food is not available.

STR: 30 **AG:** 22 **INT:** 7 **WIS:** 7 **CH:** 6 **CON:** 30
END: 60 **WILL:** 14 **POWER:** NA **CC:** 400 units
MR: 10 **Hit Points:** 30 -120 max. **Size:** 8 - 12'
MA: 10'/220'/440'/110'
Attacks: Claws 2**d10**, Bite 1**d8**, Hug 2**d10**+5 crushing
CBP: 5000 **AC:** 3

Boar

Wild boars are extremely aggressive and territorial. They have strong tusk, and move rapidly in spite of their large size. Many unwary hunters have been killed by wild boars.

STR: 15 **AG:** 24 **INT:** 4 **WIS:** 4 **CH:** 4 **CON:** 15
END: 30 **WILL:** 8 **POWER:** NA **CC:** 150 units
MR:10 **Hit Points:** 15 - 40 max. **Size:** 3 - 6'
MA: 4'/96'/192'/48'
Attacks: Tusks 1**d8**+2, Hooves 1**d6**+2
CBP: 1000 **AC:** 3

Camel

The Camel is an herbivorous desert beast used by many desert peoples for transportation. They store fat and moisture in humps on their backs and can go long distances without food or water.

STR: 30 **AG:** 18 **INT:** 5 **WIS:** 5 **CH:** 4 **CON:** 30
END: 70 **WILL:** 10 **POWER:** NA **CC:** 400 units
MR: 10 **Hit Points:** 20 - 80 max. **Size:** 8 -10'
MA: 8'/144'/288'/72'
Attacks: Hooves 1**d8** blunt, Bite 1**d4**
CBP: 500 **AC:** 3

Cat

The common domestic cat is a popular familiar for **Spellcasters**. Small, fast, and intelligent, this animal makes a good companion. Cats have *Night Vision* to 120'.

STR: 3 **AG:** 30 **INT:** 7 **WIS:** 7 **CH:** 10 **CON:** 5
END: 15 **WILL:** 20 **POWER:** NA **CC:** 5 units
MR: 2 **Hit Points:** 5 -15 max. **Size:**1 - 1'6"
MA: 2'/60'/120'/30'
Attacks: Claws 1**d4**, Bite 1**d4**
CBP: 100 **AC:** 0

Hunting Cat

The Hunting Cat is a larger cat trained for use by hunters. These cats are silent and swift. Most are gray or black with orange spots. They have *Night Vision* to 120'.

STR: 8 **AG:** 32 **INT:** 8 **WIS:** 8 **CH:** 10 **CON:** 8
END: 30 **WILL:** 24 **POWER:** NA **CC:** 30 units
MR: 5 **Hit Points:** 12 - 34 max. **Size:** 3 - 4'
MA: 4'/128'/256'/64'
Attacks: Claws 1**d8**, Bite 1**d6**
CBP: 500 **AC:** 2

Crocodile

The crocodile is a fierce reptile found in swamps, rivers, or streams. It has short legs, a powerful tail, and large snapping jaws. They are often found in groups and try to attack prey in the water rather than on land.

STR: 8 **AG:** 18 **INT:** 3 **WIS:** 3 **CH:** 4 **CON:** 10
END: 20 **WILL:** 10 **POWER:** NA **CC:** 100 units
MR: 5 **Hit Points:** 10 - 30 max. **Size:** 8 - 10'
MA: 8'/144'/288'/72' (144'/288' in water)
Attacks: Bite 1**d8** drowning
CBP: 500 **AC:** 8

Deer

The deer is a gentle, graceful herbivore found in forests, hills, meadows, and plains. The males or *bucks* have branching horns. Deer will always try to flee rather than fight.

STR: 20 **AG:**30 **INT:** 4 **WIS:** 4 **CH:** 10 **CON:** 20
END: 60 **WILL:** 8 **POWER:** NA **CC:** 300 units
MR: 5 **Hit Points:** 20 - 60 max. **Size:** 5 - 6'
MA: 6'/180'/360'/90'
Attacks: Hooves 1**d6**, Horns 1**d8**, Bite 1**d4**
CBP: 200 **AC:** 2

Dog

Differing breeds of dogs have been used by Mankind for centuries. They are smart, easily trained, and very loyal creatures. The connection between Man and Dog seems almost mystical in some instances, and dogs will almost always be found in towns, villages, or cities.

STR: 5 **AG:** 25 **INT:** 7 **WIS:** 7 **CH:** 10 **CON:** 10 **END:** 30 **WILL:** 14 **POWER:** NA **CC:** 20 units **MR:** 5 **Hit Points:** 8 - 20 max. **Size:** 2 - 4'
MA: 4'/100'/200'/50'
Attacks: Bite 1**d8**, Claw 1**d4**
CBP: 100 **AC:** 1

Hunting Dog

Hunting Dogs are bred to be slightly larger and faster than other dogs. Hunting dogs are a common animal in humanoid societies.

STR: 7 **AG:** 30 **INT:** 7 **WIS:** 8 **CH:** 12 **CON:** 12 **END:** 35 **WILL:** 20 **POWER:** NA **CC:** 30 units **MR:** 8 **Hit Points:** 10 - 25 max. **Size:** 3 - 5'
MA: 4'/120'/240'/60'
Attacks: Bite 1**d8**, Claw 1**d6**
CBP: 150 **AC:** 2

War/Watch Dog

War/Watch Dogs are bred for size and aggressiveness. These beasts are smart and dangerous.

STR: 10 **AG:** 30 **INT:** 8 **WIS:** 8 **CH:** 10 **CON:**12 **END:** 40 **WILL:** 30 **POWER:** NA **CC:** 150 units **MR:** 10 **Hit Points:** 15 - 40 max. **Size:** 3 - 6'
MA: 5'/150'/300'/75'
Attacks: Bite 1**d10**, Claw 1**d8**
CBP: 200 **AC:** 2

Eagle

Eagles are large birds of prey found mostly in mountain ranges. Eagles have remarkable eyesight and can see small creatures on the ground from a height of thousands of feet. The Eagle has strong claws or *talons* for capturing prey and a strong beak for ripping its victim into edible chunks.

STR: 5 **AG:** 22/10 **INT:** 5 **WIS:** 5 **CH:** 10 **CON:** 10 **END:** 20 **WILL:** 10 **POWER:** NA **CC:** 20 units **Hit Points:** 5 - 20 max. **MR:** 5 **Size:** 3 - 4' body **MA:** 3'/30'/60'/15' 66'/132' in flight.
Attacks: Claws1**d8**, Beak 1**d8**
CBP: 200 **AC:** 1

Eel

The eel is sometimes called the water snake. Like snakes, they are long, slender creatures with no limbs. The eel propels itself through the water by wiggling its flattened body, which is lined on both sides with a fin.

STR: 3 **AG:** 25 **INT:** 3 **WIS:** 3 **CH:** 3 **CON:** 10 **END:** 15 **WILL:** 6 **POWER:** NA **CC:** 30 units **Hit Points:** 5 - 10 max. **MR:** 5 **Size:** 3 - 6'
MA: 4'/100'/200'/50'
Attacks: Bite 1**d4**, Poison (save vs. **CON** +10, or cramps and nausea for 1**d6** hours.), Electric Charge 1**d8** electrical damage 1/10 Move
CBP: 200 **AC:** 2

Elephant

The elephant is a large herd animal used by some races for transportation and labor. They have a long, flexible trunk which they can use to manipulate objects. They also have tusks which they can use for defense.

STR: 40 **AG:** 20 **INT:** 7 **WIS:** 7 **CH:** 8 **CON:** 30 **END:** 70 **WILL:** 14 **POWER:** NA **CC:** 600 units **Hit Points:** 30 -150 max. **MR:** 10 **Size:** 12 -15' at shoulder **MA:** 10'/200'/400'/100'
Attacks: Trunk 1**d6**, Trample 3**d10**, Tusk 1**d8**
CBP: 4000 **AC:** 4

War Elephant

War Elephants are bred for aggressiveness and intelligence.

STR: 42 **AG:** 22 **INT:** 8 **WIS:** 8 **CH:** 8 **CON:** 35 **END:** 80 **WILL:** 20 **POWER:** NA **CC:** 700 units **Hit Points:** 40 - 200 max. **MR:** 10 **Size:** 15 - 20' at shoulder **MA:** 12'/264'/528'/132'
Attacks: Trunk 1**d8**, Trample 3**d10**+5, Tusk 1**d8**+2
CBP: 10000 **AC:** 5

Woolly Elephant

Woolly Elephants are found only in colder climates. They have the same statistics as the War Elephant, but are not as aggressive.

Elk

The Elk is similar in many ways to the deer, only larger in overall size. Reindeer, Caribou, and Elk are all of similar size and use the same statistics for game purposes.

STR: 30 **AG:** 20 **INT:** 5 **WIS:** 5 **CH:** 8 **CON:** 30 **END:** 60 **WILL:** 10 **POWER:** NA **CC:** 400 units **Hit Points:** 20 - 90 max. **MR:** 8 **Size** 6 - 8'
MA: 6'/120'/240'/60'
Attacks: Hooves 1**d10**, Horns 1**d8**, Bite 1**d6**
CBP: 500 **AC:** 3

Fox

The Fox is a small, smart, and aggressive member of the canine family. Foxes often live near Man and are good hunters of small prey.

STR: 4 **AG:** 35 **INT:** 9 **WIS:** 9 **CH:** 10 **CON:** 10 **END:** 25 **WILL:** 20 **POWER:** NA **CC:** 10 units **Hit Points:** 5 -18 max. **MR:** 2 **Size:** 2-3'length
MA: 3'/105'/210'/53'
Attacks: Bite 1**d6**, Claw 1**d4**
CBP: 100 **AC:** 0

Hawk

The Hawk is a medium-sized bird of prey. It is fast and maneuverable in the air and often feeds on smaller birds and small mammals. Hawks are frequently kept by nobles as pets and are used to hunt for sport.

STR: 2 **AG:** 25 **INT:** 5 **WIS:** 5 **CH:** 12 **CON:** 10 **END:** 15 **WILL:** 10 **POWER:** NA **CC:** 10 units **MR:** 5 **Hit Points:** 5 - 15 max. **Size:** 1 - 2' **MA:** 2'/50'/100'/25' (100'/200' in flight). **Attacks:** Claws 1**d4**, Beak 1**d4** **CBP:** 100 **AC:** 1

Hunting and War Hawks use the same statistics as the Common Eagle.

Horse

The Horse is a common domesticated herd beast, used by humanoids for transportation and labor.

STR: 40 **AG:** 20 **INT:** 4 **WIS:** 4 **CH:**10 **CON:** 30 **END:** 70 **WILL:** 8 **POWER:** NA **CC:** 500 units **MR:** 10 **Hit Points:** 20 - 85 max. **Size:** 5 - 6'at shoulder **MA:** 6'/120'/240'/60' **Attacks:** Hooves 1**d10**, Bite 1**d6** **CBP:** 500 **AC:** 3

This class includes all Riding and Pack Horses.

Mule

Mules are not really Horses, but are a similar herd beast often used as pack animals.

STR: 35 **AG:** 20 **INT:** 4 **WIS:** 4 **CH:** 8 **CON:** 30 **END:** 65 **WILL:** 20 **POWER:** NA **CC:** 400 units **MR:** 15 **Hit Points:** 20 - 80 max. **Size:** 3 - 4' at shoulder **MA:** 4'/80'/160'/40' **Attacks:** Hooves 1**d8**, Bite 1**d6** **CBP:** 500

Pony

The Pony is a smaller version of the Horse. These sturdy little beasts are often used by the smaller races instead of Horses.

STR: 35 **AG:** 20 **INT:** 6 **WIS:** 6 **CH:**10 **CON:** 30 **END:** 65 **WILL:** 12 **POWER:** NA **CC:** 400 units **MR:** 10 **Hit Points:** 20 - 80 max. **Size:** 3 - 4' at shoulder **MA:** 4'/80'/160'/40' **Attacks:** Hooves 1**d8**, Bite1**d6** **CBP:** 500

War Horse

War Horses are similar to other Horses, only larger in size and mass. They have been trained to fight in combat with their rider.

STR: 45 **AG:** 30 **INT:** 6 **WIS:** 6 **CH:**10 **CON:** 30 **END:** 80 **WILL:** 15 **POWER:** NA **CC:** 600 units **MR:** 20 **Hit Points:** 30 -120 max. **Size:** 6 - 8' at shoulder **MA:** 7'/210'/420'/105' **Attacks:** Hooves 2**d8**, Bite 1**d8** **CBP:** 2000 **AC:** 4

Hyena

The Hyena is a fierce hunter/scavenger that travels in packs. It is dog-like in appearance, with spotted fur and bone-crushing jaws.

STR: 10 **AG:** 25 **INT:** 6 **WIS:** 6 **CH:** 6 **CON:** 20 **END:** 30 **WILL:** 12 **POWER:** NA **CC:** 100 units **MR:** 5 **Hit Points:** 12 - 30 max. **Size:** 3' **MA:** 3'/45'/90'/23' **Attacks:** Claws 1**d6**, Bite 1**d10** **CBP:** 200 **AC:** 4

Leech

The Leech is a parasite that feeds on blood. They are found in ponds, rivers, and streams. They are small -- often less than 3" in length -- and look like garden slugs. Salt is often used to kill them. Removing them forceably can create wounds which can to become infected.

STR: .01 **AG:** 20 **INT:** 1 **WIS:** 1 **CH:** 0 **CON:** 5 **END:** 5 **WILL:** 2 **POWER:** NA **CC:** .1 unit **MR:** 1 **Hit Points:** 1max. **Size:** 1- 3" **MA:** 1"/20"/40"/10" **Attacks:** Bite 1pt. **CBP:**1 **AC:** 0

Lion

The Lion is a large predatory Cat found mostly on the plains. They travel in large groups called *prides*. Male Lions have manes; females do not. The females of a pride are the hunters under normal circumstances, and can take down much larger animals.

STR: 30 **AG:** 30 **INT:** 7 **WIS:** 7 **CH:** 8 **CON:** 20 **END:** 60 **WILL:** 20 **POWER:** NA **CC:** 400 units **MR :** 8 **Hit Points:** 20 - 100 max. **Size:** 3 - 4' at shoulder **MA:** 4'/120'/240'/60' **Attacks:** Claws 1**d8**+2, Bite 1**d6** **CBP:** 500 **AC:** 3

Lynx

The Lynx is another large Cat. They hunt small mammals and birds for the bulk of their diet. The Lynx is found in almost all woodland areas.

STR: 20 **AG:** 30 **INT:** 7 **WIS:** 7 **CH:**10 **CON:** 20 **END:** 50 **WILL:** 20 **POWER:** NA **CC:** 300 units **MR:** 8 **Hit Points:** 15 - 60 max. **Size:** 3 - 4' length **MA:** 4'/120'/240'/60' **Attacks:** Claws 1**d6**+2, Bite 1**d6** **CBP:** 500 **AC:** 2

Octopus

The Octopus is a relatively intelligent saltwater invertebrate. It has a bulbous main body and eight radiating, highly flexible tentacles. The Octopus is a predator/scavenger with amazing strength and speed.

STR:10 **AG:** 30 **INT:**10 **WIS:**10 **CH:** 5 **CON:** 20 **END:** 30 **WILL:** 20 **POWER:** NA **CC:** 100 units **MR:** 5 **Hit Points:** 5 - 20 max.**Size:** 2 - 5' length
MA: 4'/120'/240'/60'
Attacks: Hug 1**d8** crushing, Bite 1**d4**
CBP: 100 **AC:** 0

Giant Octopus

The Giant Octopus is found in the deeper waters of the open ocean. It is much larger than the Common Octopus, and some have been known to attack whales or small ships.

STR: 30 **AG:** 30 **INT:**10 **WIS:**10 **CH:** 5 **CON:** 30 **END:** 60 **WILL:** 20 **POWER:** NA **CC:** 800 units **MR:** 15 **Hit Points:** 30 -90 max. body, 10 - 40 max. tentacles **Size:** 25 -150' length
MA: 50'/1500'/3000'/750'
Attacks: Hug **4d10** crushing, Bite **1d12+8**
CBP: 10000 **AC:** 4

Otter

The Otter is a small mammal that lives a large part of its life in the water. It eats fish, insects, and some plants as the bulk of its diet.

STR: 4 **AG:** 30 **INT:** 7 **WIS** :7 **CH:** 10 **CON:** 10 **END:** 20 **WILL:** 15 **POWER:** NA **CC:** 20 units **MR:** 2 **Hit Points:** 2 -10 max. **Size:** 2 - 3' length
MA: 2'/60'/120'/30'
Attacks: Claws 2pts., Bite 1**d4**
CBP: 50 **AC:** 1

Owl

This is a mid-sized, night-flying bird of prey. The Owl has *Night Vision* to 600' and flies silently.

STR: 5 **AG:** 25 **INT:** 6 **WIS:** 6 **CH:** 10 **CON:** 10 **END:** 20 **WILL:** 12 **POWER:** NA **CC:** 15 units **MR:** 0 **Hit Points:** 2 -15 max. **Size:** 1- 3' length
MA: 3'/75'/150'/38'
Attacks: Claws 1**d8**, Beak 1**d4**
CBP: 50 **AC:** 2

Panther (Leopard)

The Panther is a large predatory Cat, found in woodlands, mountains, and swamps. It is found in a wide range of climates and is primarily a solitary hunter. *Move Silently* is a natural ability for this large Cat.

STR: 25 **AG:** 32 **INT:** 7 **WIS:** 7 **CH:** 12 **CON:** 20 **END:** 50 **WILL:** 20 **POWER:** NA **CC:** 350 units **MR:** 4 **Hit Points:** 20 - 90 max. **Size:** 4 - 6'length **MA:** 6'/192'/384'/96'
Attacks: Claws 1**d8+2**, Bite 1**d6**
CBP: 200 **AC:** 3

Peacock

The Peacock is a colorful bird sought for its beautiful plumage. The Peacock is not a smart animal nor is it hostile. They are often kept as pets on large estates.

STR: 1 **AG:** 14 **INT:** 4 **WIS:** 4 **CH:** 10 **CON:** 10 **END:** 12 **WILL:** 8 **POWER:** NA **CC:** 5 units **MR:** 1 **Hit Points:** 2 - 6 max. **Size:** 1- 2' body
MA: 2'/28'/56'/14'
Attacks: Claws 1pt., Beak 2pts.
CBP: 10 **AC:** 1

Quail (Pheasant/Small Game Birds)

The Quail is a small game bird often hunted for food. It is nonaggressive and only capable of inflicting slight damage. Other game birds include: Pheasant, Duck, Goose, and Chickens. All use the same statistics for game play.

STR: 2 **AG:** 25 **INT:** 3 **WIS:** 3 **CH:** 10 **CON:** 10 **END:** 12 **WILL:** 6 **POWER:** NA **CC:** 4 units **MR:** 1 **Hit Points:** 2 - 8 max. **Size:** 8"-1' body
MA: 1'/25'/50'/13' 100' in flight
Attacks: Claws 1pt., Beak 1pt.
CBP: 20 **AC:** 1

Rat

This small rodent is found in almost every climate. They are fast, highly adaptable mammals, capable of eating just about anything. They are also carriers of many harmful diseases. Rats should be avoided whenever possible, no matter what their size.

STR: 1 **AG:** 35 **INT:** 6 **WIS:** 6 **CH:** 2 **CON:** 15 **END:** 20 **WILL:** 15 **POWER:** NA **CC:** 1 unit **MR:** 1 **Hit Points:** 1- 4 max. **Size:** 6"-1' body
MA: 1'/35'/70'/18'
Attacks: Claws 2pts., Bite 2pts. (save vs. **CON** from any wound or get a disease)
CBP: 10 **AC:** 0

Ram (Goats/Sheep)

The Ram is a relatively harmless herd beast unless provoked. It has large horns that spiral backward, which it uses to attack or defend. Goats have upward-pointing horns. Sheep have no horns.

STR: 6 **AG:** 20 **INT:** 4 **WIS:** 4 **CH:** 6 **CON:** 20 **END:** 30 **WILL:** 8 **POWER:** NA **CC:** 60 units **MR:** 5 **Hit Points:** 6- 20 max. **Size:** 3- 4' length
MA: 4'/80'/160'/40' (no Mountain Terrain penalties).
Attacks: Horns 1**d6**, Kick 1**d6**, Bite 1**d4**
CBP: 100 **AC:** 2

Raven

The Raven is a large black bird often used by **Spellcasters** as a familiar. Crows are capable of limited speech.

STR: 2 **AG:** 20 **INT:** 8 **WIS:** 8 **CH:** 8 **CON:** 10
END: 15 **WILL:** 20 **POWER:** NA **CC:** 2 units
MR: 1 **Hit Points:** 2- 8 max. **Size:** 1'-1'6" body
Attacks: Claws 1**d4**, Beak 1**d4**
CBP: 100 **AC:** 2

Salamander (Newt)

This small snake-like amphibious Lizard is often used as a component in ritual spells and potions. It is a harmless creature and will flee if attacked.

STR: 1 **AG:** 30 **INT:** 2 **WIS:** 2 **CH:** 3 **CON:** 5
END: 8 **WILL:** 4 **POWER:** NA **CC:** .2 unit
MR: 0 **Hit Points:** 1 max. **Size:** 3 - 5" length
MA: 2"/5'/10'/2'6"
Attacks: None
CBP: .5 **AC:** 0

Shark

The Shark is essentially a mindless feeding machine, found primarily in saltwater. They will attack Man, and are drawn to the scent of blood in water. They can detect blood in water even from small wounds as far as 3 miles away.

STR: 8 **AG:** 30 **INT:** 1 **WIS:** 1 **CH:** 1 **CON:** 20
END: 30 **WILL:** 2 **POWER:** NA **CC:** 80 units
MR: 5 **Hit Points:** 10 - 30 max. **Size:** 4 - 10' length **MA:** 6'/180'/360'/90'
Attacks: Bite 2**d10**
CBP: 500 **AC:** 3

Snake

There are numerous types of Snakes in the world, far too many to list them all separately. For **Webs** purposes we have limited them to three kinds.

Common Snake

Common Snakes are nonvenomous reptiles. They are not very big and are relatively harmless.

STR: 1 **AG:** 30 **INT:** 2 **WIS:** 2 **CH:** 4 **CON:** 10
END: 15 **WILL:** 4 **POWER:** NA **CC:** 1 unit
MR: 2 **Hit Points:** 1- 8 max. **Size:** 2 - 4' length
MA: 2'/60'/120'/30'
Attacks: Bite 1**d4**
CBP: 50 **AC:** 2

Constricting Snake

Constricting Snakes are large, powerful reptiles which can grow to be quite long. The largest ever recorded was an anaconda 150' long discovered on a satellite photo, but such large sizes are extremely rare.

STR: 20 **AG:** 30 **INT:** 2 **WIS:** 2 **CH:** 4 **CON:** 10
END: 15 **WILL:** 4 **POWER:** NA **CC:** 200 units
MR: 5 **Hit Points:** 16 - 58 max. **Size:** 6 - 25' length **MA:** 6'/180'/360'/90'
Attacks: Bite 1**d8**
CBP: 500 **AC:** 5

Poisonous Snake

Poisonous Snakes/Vipers are relatively small, like Common Snakes, but can inject poison when they bite. The **GM** should decide how strong these venoms are and what saves will be necessary. Most bites should cause severe illness or death (example: Coral Snakes: save vs **CON** +10 or Death).

STR: 1 **AG:** 30 **INT:** 2 **WIS:** 2 **CH:** 4 **CON:** 10
END: 15 **WILL:** 4 **POWER:** NA **CC:** 1 unit
MR: 2 **Hit Points:** 1- 8 max. **Size:** 2 -4' length
MA: 2'/60'/120'/30'
Attacks: Bite 1**d6** , Poison (special)
CBP: 50 **AC:** 2

Tiger

The Tiger is another of the large predatory Cats. It has a characteristic black and orange, or white and black stripe pattern not seen in other Cats. Tigers *Move Silently* and *Hide/Blend* in rocks /shadows/undergrowth. They also have *Night Vision* to 100'.

STR: 30 **AG:** 36 **INT:** 7 **WIS:** 7 **CH:** 12
CON: 30 **END:** 65 **WILL:** 20 **POWER:** NA
CC 300 units **MR:** 8 **Hit Points:** 18 - 70 max.
Size: 2 - 4' at shoulder **MA:** 6'/216'/432'/108'
Attacks: Claws 1**d10**, Bite 1**d6**
CBP: 2000 **AC:** 2

Turtle

The Turtle is a slow-moving reptile with a hard armored shell. They are usually small and harmless creatures, although some species have been known to grow quite large.

STR: 5 **AG:** 8 **INT:** 4 **WIS:** 4 **CH:** 8 **CON:** 30
END: 35 **WILL:** 10 **POWER:** NA **CC:** 10 units
MR: 8 **Hit Points:** 1- 10 max. **Size:** 1 - 2' length
MA:1'/8'/16'/4'
Attacks: Bite 1pt.
CBP: 20 **AC:** 5 (shell)

Snapping Turtle

The SnappingTurtle is a more aggressive breed of Turtle. They have strong crushing jaws that are capable of breaking bones.

STR: 5 **AG:** 8 **INT:** 4 **WIS:** 4 **CH:** 8 **CON:** 30
END: 35 **WILL:** 10 **POWER:** NA **CC:** 10 units
MR: 8 **Hit Points:** 1-10 max. **Size:** 1- 2' length
MA:1'/8'/16'/4'
Attacks: Bite 1**d10**
CBP: 50 **AC:** 5 (shell)

Vulture

The Vulture is a large scavenger bird which feeds on carrion. Dead creatures can often be found by watching for circling Vultures.
STR: 3 **AG:** 25 **INT:** 3 **WIS:** 3 **CH:** 4 **CON:** 30 **END:** 35 **WILL:** 10 **POWER:** NA **CC:** 3 units **MR:** 8 **Hit Points:** 8 - 12 max. **Size:** 2 - 4' body **MA:**4'/100'/200'/50', 400' in flight
Attacks: Claws 1**d6**, Beak 1**d6**
CBP: 100 **AC:** 2

Weasel (Ferret/ Mongoose)

This is a small, thin, snake-like mammal that eats insects, small mammals, snakes, and small birds. Its slender body allows it to enter burrow holes and nests with ease.
STR: 2 **AG:** 36 **INT:** 7 **WIS:** 7 **CH:** 12 **CON:** 30 **END:** 32 **WILL:** 20 **POWER:** NA **CC:** 6 units **MR:** 8 **Hit Points:** 2 - 8 max. **Size:** 1 - 2' length **MA:**1'/36'/64'/18'
Attacks: Claws 1**d4**, Bite 1**d4**
CBP: 100 **AC:** 0

Whale

The Whale is a large sea-dwelling mammal. Most Whales feed on plankton or small fish and are quite harmless to Man. Their large size has led to the mistaken belief that they sometimes eat ships. Although this is untrue, some species such as Killer Whales will eat Men, thinking they are Seals.
STR: 80 **AG:** 20 **INT:** 10 **WIS:**10 **CH:**12 **CON:** 30 **END:** 120 **WILL:** 40 **POWER:** NA **CC:**1000 units **MR:** 20 **Hit Points:** 40 -250 max. **Size:** 30-50' length **MA:** 20'/400'/800'/200'
Attacks: Bite 1**d10**, Ram 4**d10**, Tail Bash 4**d20**
CBP: 10000 **AC:** 5

Wolf

This is a large predatory canine. The hearing and sense of smell possessed by Wolves is much better than that of humans (200' range), so it is almost impossible to suprise them. Wolves tend to hunt in packs and will bring down very large game. Wolves *Move Silently*, and *Hide/Blend* in rocks, shadows, and undergrowth.
STR: 12 **AG:** 32 **INT:** 8 **WIS:** 8 **CH:** 12 **CON:** 30 **END:** 50 **WILL:** 30 **POWER:** NA **CC:** 150 units **MR:** 10 **Hit Points:** 16 - 42 max. **Size:** 3 - 6' length **MA:** 6'/192'/384'/96'
Attacks: Claws 1**d8**, Bite 1**d10**
CBP: 200 **AC:** 3

War Wolf

This is a larger version of the Common Wolf, bred for strength. Some races use them as soldiers or for mounts.
STR: 15 **AG:** 32 **INT:** 8 **WIS:** 8 **CH:** 12 **CON:** 30 **END:** 60 **WILL:** 30 **POWER:** NA **CC:** 180 units **MR:** 10 **Hit Points:** 16 - 42 max. **Size:** 6-8' length **MA:** 6'/192'/384'/96'
Attacks: Claws 1**d10**, Bite 1**d12**
CBP: 1000 **AC:** 3

Sample Characters and Gamemaster Notes

Sample Characters

By now you're probably more than a little confused. It seems to involve so *much* to make a Character for your gaming. However, it really isn't as difficult as all this manual might make it first appear.

To give you a better idea of what to expect, we've taken a couple of familiar fictional Characters and broken them down for you to look at:

ROBIN HOOD (Sir Robin of Locksley)

Archetype: Weaponmaster (Archer)

Prime Attributes

STR: 10	**AG:** 14 (20) 60**BP**	**INT:** 15
WIS: 12	**CH:** 12	**CON:** 10
VC: 11		

Secondary Attributes

PCP: 27	**END:** 20	**WILL:** 27
LUCK: 39	**CNC:** 27	**POWER:** 37
PSP: 37	**CC:** 120 units	**MR:** 5
Hit Points: 16		

Buy Points

At Beginning:	2000**BP**
Disadvantages:	700**BP**
Total:	2700**BP**
Amount Spent:	2692**BP**
Earned:	0**BP**
End Total:	8**BP**

Disadvantages

Hunted(Sir Guy of Gisborne)	100**BP**
Enemy(Sheriff of Nottingham)	500**BP**
Dependent(Maid Marian)	50**BP**
Loyalty to Friends(strong/common)	50**BP**

Childhood Skills (CHS):

Read/Write English	(95%)
Animal Lore	(97%)
Animal Riding/4-legged	(100%)
Heraldry	(95%)

Character Skills:

Chess	(90%)	1**BP**
Horse Breeding	(90%)	1**BP**

Life Skills:

Balance	(60%)	20**BP**
Acrobatics	(60%)	30**BP**
Charm/Con	(52%)	20**BP**
Performance	(57%)	10**BP**
Acting	(52%)	50**BP**
Aiming	(52%)	10**BP**
Alertness	(57%)	20**BP**
Dodge/Parry	(60%)	60**BP**
Anticipate Blow		30**BP**
Anticipate Dodge	(52%)	30**BP**
Appraising	(52%)	30**BP**
Bowyer/Fletcher	(52%)	20**BP**
Brawling	(60%)	20**BP**
Climbing	(60%)	20**BP**
Disguise	(52%)	30**BP**
Fast Aim	(60%)	50**BP**
Fast Draw	(60%)	50**BP**
Fast Load	(60%)	50**BP**
Following	(57%)	50**BP**
Plant Lore	(52%)	20**BP**
Foraging	(52%)	10**BP**
Hide/Blend	(52%)	50**BP**
Hunting	(52%)	40**BP**
Leadership	(52%)	50**BP**
Mounted Fighting	(60%)	50**BP**
Move Silently	(60%)	40**BP**
Open Locks	(60%)	50**BP**
Rope Mastery	(60%)	30**BP**
Running Sprint	(60%)	60**BP**
Search	(57%)	50**BP**
Swimming	(60%)	20**BP**
Trap Setting/Disarming	(52%)	50**BP**
Two Handed Fighting	(60%)	50**BP**
Blades	(60%)	30**BP**
Bows	(50%)	30**BP**
Weapon Mastery/Bows		30**BP**
Long Dagger	(100%)	150**BP**
Long Sword	(100%)	150**BP**
Hunting Bow	(110%)	330**BP**
Hunting Bow II	(100%)	280**BP**
Hunting Bow III	(100%)	280**BP**
Hunting Bow IV	(80%)	130**BP**

Note: *The Agility score was bought up from 14 to 20 points. Buying* Hunting Bow *4 times allows the player to add +4 to damage, have 4 attacks (if he makes his fast loads), or make trick shots which require a Level 4 skill (i.e., splitting the shaft of another arrow). Also note that the player has not used all available Creation Points. These can be converted into gold pieces, or they can be used like luck to change die rolls. Once spent they are not regained, but new points can be earned.)*

Now the Gamemaster should assist in equipping the Character and in detailing the Character's appearance.

SHERLOCK HOLMES

Archetype: Rogue (Detective)

Prime Attributes

STR: 10 **AG:** 10(16) 60**BP**
INT: 20(25) 100**BP** **WIS:** 20(25) 100**BP**
CH: 12 **CON:** 10 **VC:** 10

Secondary Attributes

PCP: 50 **END:** 20 **WILL:** 50
LUCK: 52 **CNC:** 50 **POWER:** 50
PSP: 50 **CC:** 120 units **MR:** 5
Hit Points: 16

Buy Points

At Beginning:	2000**BP**
Disadvantages:	1020**BP**
Total:	3020**BP**
Amount Spent:	3037**BP**
Earned:	0**BP**
End Total:	-17**BP**

Disadvantages

Enemy (Dr. Moriarity)	800**BP**
Dependent (Dr. Watson)	50**BP**
Loyalty to friends(strong/common)	50**BP**
Heroin Addiction(Impaired **INT/WIS**,1 per day/uncommon/expensive)	50**BP**
Obsessive need to discover the truth(total/common)	70**BP**

Childhood Skills (CHS):

Read/Write English	(105%)
Math	(105%)
Brawling	(96%)
Charm/Con	(92%)

Character Skills:

Musician/Violin	(90%)	1**BP**
Bicycle	(90%)	1**BP**

Life Skills:

Performance	(80%)	10**BP**
Acting	(52%)	50**BP**
Administration	(65%)	20**BP**
Aiming	(65%)	10**BP**
Alertness	(100%)	60**BP**
Anatomy/Human	(65%)	20**BP**
Anatomy/Animal	(65%)	20**BP**
Animal Identification	(65%)	30**BP**
Animal Lore	(80%)	30**BP**
Animal Riding/4-legged	(56%)	50**BP**
Anthropology	(65%)	30**BP**
Dodge/Parry	(76%)	160**BP**
Anticipate Blow		30**BP**
Anticipate Dodge	(65%)	30**BP**
Appraising	(65%)	30**BP**
Balance	(56%)	20**BP**
Barter/Fence	(52%)	30**BP**
Plant Lore	(65%)	20**BP**
Biology	(65%)	30**BP**
Chemistry	(65%)	30**BP**
Biochemistry	(65%)	30**BP**
Bluff/Bribe	(80%)	20**BP**
Boating	(65%)	20**BP**
Body Language Interp.	(65%)	20**BP**
Sleight of Hand	(56%)	50**BP**
Conceal Object/Weapon	(65%)	40**BP**
Criminology	(100%)	135**BP**
Language Lore	(65%)	40**BP**
Cryptography	(80%)	20**BP**
Demolition	(65%)	30**BP**
Detect Lie	(80%)	20**BP**
Direction Sense	(65%)	40**BP**
Disguise	(65%)	30**BP**
Fast Aim	(56%)	50**BP**
Fast Draw	(56%)	50**BP**
Fast Load	(56%)	50**BP**
Following	(80%)	50**BP**
Forensics	(65%)	30**BP**
Geology	(65%)	30**BP**
Gauging	(65%)	20**BP**
Hand-to-Hand	(56%)	50**BP**
Heraldry	(65%)	10**BP**
Hide/Blend	(65%)	50**BP**
History/General	(65%)	20**BP**
Hunting	(65%)	40**BP**
Interrogation	(100%)	130**BP**
Law	(65%)	30**BP**
Library Use	(65%)	30**BP**
Literature	(65%)	30**BP**
Make/Use Poison	(65%)	50**BP**
Map Making	(65%)	40**BP**
Memorize	(65%)	20**BP**
Move Silently	(56%)	40**BP**
Open Locks	(56%)	50**BP**
Running Sprint	(70%)	80**BP**
Search	(100%)	150**BP**
Speed Reading	(65%)	20**BP**
Guns	(56%)	30**BP**
Haymaker	(50%)	10**BP**
Roundhouse	(70%)	110**BP**
Boxing	(50%)	10**BP**
Body Slam	(50%)	10**BP**
.357 Revolver	(100%)	250**BP**
Swimming	(56%)	20**BP**

Note:* *AG*, *INT*, *and* *WIS *have all been bought up, but the* ***LUCK*** *score remains the same. Sherlock Holmes is a skill-heavy Character, as literature implies, and therefore has a large number of strong disadvantages to compensate for this. You will notice he currently has a negative Buy Point score. This will be used against him as bad luck by the* ***GM*** *during play. He can, however, buy off the bad luck whenever he wishes or can afford to at a 2pt. per 1pt. ratio.*

As you can see, any Character can be translated into a ***Webs Gaming System*** *Character. It is the* ***GM****'s job to use the Character's disadvantages against him or her. It is* ***not*** *(and we emphasize this) the* ***GM****'s job to* ***kill off*** *Characters. The* ***GM*** *needs to keep the game challenging and interesting, and under normal circumstances some Characters may die during play, but the* ***GM*** *should not deliberately try to kill off the Characters. That isn't fun for anyone.*

Advancing Characters

As you play, the *Gamemaster* will award points to your Character for various actions, such as slaying monsters, using skills, good role-playing or just plain good manners.

"Earned" *Buy Points* can then be used to enhance your Character, either by increasing skill levels or buying new skills. This should only be done between playing sessions or when you and the other players are in a play area where you could realistically work on such skills in a real-life setting. As a last comment on this subject, it's always good to keep a record of how many *Buy Points* you've earned and how many have been spent on Character development.

A Note to GameMasters

Being a *Gamemaster* can be difficult because it's up to you to create the game world. You must make it flexible and challenging and be able to react to the unexpected actions of players.

Try to incorporate as much detail as you can into each game session and not get bogged down in rolling dice. Each game module will have notes and suggestions for the *Gamemaster*, but these are only suggestions; it's your campaign, and you can use whatever rules you wish to use. Just be sure you stick to those rules once you've set them up.

Assigning *Buy Points* is the *Gamemaster's* primary job. In **Webs,** every 2000**BP** = 1**BP** level. To assign credit for defeating a Monster or Creature, divide the Creature's *Buy Points* for Creation by the Player's **BP** level. This equals the *Buy Points* awarded for the creature's defeat. If this number is less than 1, no *Buy Points* are earned.

When attacking multiple Creatures, add together the *Creation* **BP** of all the defeated Creatures, then divide by the Player's **BP** level. If multiple Players attack a single Creature, then the *Creation* **BP** of the Creature is first divided by the number of attackers.

Use of skills, good role playing and innovative ideas should be rewarded with *Buy Points* as well.

You must also be able to look at the situation your Characters are in and decide what kind of bonuses or penalties a Character should have when using his or her skills. The greater the difficulty and more stressful the situation, the more penalties there should be. It is possible, in fact, to have over 100% in penalties.

You should purchase a genre supplemental resource book along with this basic game book. There are 5 **Webs** Supplemental Games: **Webs of Wizardry, Web of Stars, Web of Horrors, Web of Shadows** and **Web of Heroes**. Of course, you can create your own universes and games without purchase of any of these genre systems, but new races, technologies and powers are included in the supplements and are highly recommended.

...and so the curtain closes ...
...for now...

Interior Illustrations by

Fritzen Ravenswood
Keith Bailey
Gino Dykstra